On the Sociology
of Islam

On the Sociology of Islam

Lectures by
ALI SHARI'ATI

Translated from the Persian
by
HAMID ALGAR

MIZAN PRESS
Oneonta, New York

Shari'ati, Ali, 1933-1977.
      On the Sociology of Islam/by Ali Shari'ati;
      translated by Hamid Algar -- 1st ed.

         p. cm.
         Includes bibliographical references and index.
         LCCN 79-83552
         ISBN: 0-933782-06-3 (hbk.)
         ISBN: 0-933782-00-4 (pbk.)

         1. Sociology, Islamic 2. Man (Islam).
      I. Title

      BP173.25.S52 2000   297.27
                          QBI00-276

Director of Publications: Moin Shaikh
Cover and Book Design: Heidi Bendorf

TRANSLATOR'S FOREWORD

THE RECENT SERIES of demonstrations and uprisings against the dictatorial regime of the Shah has served to bring into renewed prominence two facts frequently overlooked by most observers of the Iranian scene: the continued loyalty to Islam of the mass of the Iranian people, and the vitality of the Iranian religious leadership in directing popular aspirations. A superficial glance at the westernized exterior of the major cities of Iran might leave the impression of one of the most radically transformed and "de-Islamized" societies in the Islamic world, but it is precisely in Iran that one of the most vital and deep-rooted movements exists for the reassertion of the political and social hegemony of Islam.

To a large extent the direction of this movement lies in the hands of the Shi'i 'ulama who, for a variety of reasons—social, historical and theological—have maintained their independence from the state and their alignment with popular feeling more effectively than many of their Sunni counterparts. But an important role has also been played by a number of intellectuals and thinkers who, especially in the post-War period, have endeavored to integrate the fruits of modern learning with traditional belief and thus evolve a new Islamic idiom capable of securing the allegiance of the secularly educated. Particularly significant in this group are Muhandis Bazargan, formerly professor at Tehran University, and Dr. Ali Shari'ati, author of the present collection.

The translated extracts from his work are preceded by a biographical sketch from the pen of one who was close to Shari'ati. We may, however, summarize here the chief facts of his life. Born in 1933 in a village near Sabzavar on the edge of the Kavir desert, he was educated first by his father, Muhammad Taqi Shari'ati, one of the foremost Iranian 'ulama of the present age. He then studied in Mashhad and simultaneously began

his career of political, social and intellectual struggle, which, in
the years of repression following the overthrow of Musaddiq,
resulted in his imprisonment for a number of months. In 1959,
he went to Paris to continue his studies in sociology and related
fields, but there too, he did not restrict himself to the conventional life of a student. He participated actively in the organization abroad of an Islamically-oriented opposition to the Shah's
regime. In 1964, he returned to Iran, but was immediately
arrested. Six months later, as a result of international pressure
on the Iranian regime, he was released and permitted to assume
a succession of teaching posts, culminating in an appointment
at the University of Mashhad. But he was compelled to resign
from the university, and there began instead what was possibly
the most creative period of his life, despite its brevity. He
lectured at the celebrated Husayniya-yi Irshad, a religious center in Tehran that succeeded in attracting overflow audiences to
its meetings and lectures on Islamic themes. In his numerous
lectures, at the Husayniya-yi Irshad and elsewhere, he pursued
the evolution of his distinctive theories on the sociology and
history of Islam, some of which are reflected in this book. Not
surprisingly, the Husayniya-yi Irshad was closed down, and
Shari'ati was imprisoned again, this time for a period of 18
months, during which he suffered severe hardship and deprivation. Shortly after his release, he went to England, dying there
under mysterious circumstances that suggest the almost certain
involvement of the Iranian secret police, on June 19, 1977. He
was buried in Damascus, next to the shrine of Hazrat Zaynab.
Rahimahullah!
    The title of the present collection, *On the Sociology of Islam,*
requires certain elucidation. The book does not pretend to offer
a complete scheme of Islamic sociology, nor did Shari'ati himself claim to have developed a complete scheme. He himself
wrote: "I never believe that what I say is the last word on the
subject; what I say now I might change or complete tomorrow."
(*Islamshinasi,* Vol. I, p. 47). With his original and courageous
mind, he did, however, put forward a number of totally fresh
concepts relating to the sociology of Islam, and it is these we
have sought to present in English translation as a stimulus to

thought among Muslims. The book contains a number of topics that are not, strictly speaking, sociological, but even they are treated in a sociological tone, so that the title of the book, *On the Sociology of Islam,* appears justified.

Most of Shari'ati's books consist of the lectures he delivered. They are marked, therefore, by a certain repetition of theme that is characteristic of lecturing style. In some cases, we have deleted or abbreviated statements that appear to be repetitious. A number of other phrases and sentences that do not affect the main theme have also been omitted for various reasons. Otherwise, the translation is an integral and faithful reflection of the original. Elucidatory footnotes added by the translator are identified with (Tr.); all other footnotes are by Shari'ati himself.

H.A.

Berkeley
Sha'ban 1398/July 1978

Contents

IN THE NAME OF GOD

Do not imagine those killed in God's path to be dead; rather they are
alive, nurtured in the presence of their Lord.

Qur'an, 3:169

Seeking refuge in history, out of fear of loneliness, I immediately sought
out my brother Ayn al-Quzat,[1] who was burned to death in the very
blossoming of his youth for the crime of awareness and sensitivity, for
the boldness of his thought. For in an age of ignorance, awareness is
itself a crime. Loftiness of spirit and fortitude of heart in the society of the
oppressed and the humiliated, and, as the Buddha said, "being an island
in a land of lakes," are unforgivable sins.

ALI SHARI'ATI, from the
introduction to *Kavir* (Desert)

INTRODUCTION
A Biobibliographical Sketch

YES, AWARENESS, sensitivity, boldness of thought, loftiness
of spirit and fortitude of heart—these were the great human
attributes that he found he had in common with Ayn al-Quzat,
and with his sharp insight, he perceived that his fate would be
like that of Ayn al-Quzat—premature death in the earliest part
of youth. It is not surprising that when he applied his insight
and perception to himself, he foresaw everything and was
unafraid to speak. But he knew that in a society composed of the
oppressed and the humiliated, in an age of ignorance, in the
desert of neglect—or, better to say, in an age that pretends to
neglect and ignore the truth—awareness and sensitivity are no
longer synonymous with boldness of thought and fortitude of
heart; on the contrary, the quality of intellectuality has become
equated with ambition and the desire for position, and is thus

---

[1] Ayn al-Quzat Hamadani: a Persian Sufi put to death in Baghdad in 526/
1132 on charges of heresy. (TR.)

in itself one cause for the oppression and humiliation of the conscious. It was he who chided and reproached with a painful smile those intellectuals who do not have the courage even to participate in corruption, who remain waiting, in perplexity and confusion, at the crossroads and who never take any examination for fear of failing. For him, the choice of a path was not the "first step"; it was the whole of life, and hesitation and doubt were the result of our present intellectual servitude, which we designate metaphorically as "intellectualism." Throughout his extremely brief but fruitful life, he struggled boldly with all his strength and capacity against this ancient and familiar enemy of thought and humanity.

At the same time, he waged a campaign of resistance against the habit of regarding the actual as normal and acceptable, instead of seeking to replace it with the ideal; against the view of human life as vain and pointless; against banality and the sense of vanity; against the morphine that has submerged, in a state halfway between sleeping and waking, in the dream of neglect and a state of uselessness, not only the overwhelming majority of the people, but even a segment of the guardians of the religion of *tauhid,* and diverted them from the path of truth, with its rises and falls—a path demanding vital faith, dynamic thought, and a wakeful conscience. He waged a constant struggle against the evil temper of our age and our society, the withered root of which can be watered only by the renunciation of all things, even life itself, by martyrdom!

> I cannot endure remaining silent and being unable to say anything. I shall remain silent, but I feel like a person enduring the pangs of death who knows that peace and salvation await him, who is tired of the troubles of life, for whom there is nothing but a waiting that lasts a whole lifetime . . . .
>
> Do you not see how sweetly and peacefully a martyr dies?
>
> For those fully accustomed to their everyday routine, death is an awesome tragedy, a horrendous cessation of all things; it is becoming lost in nothingness. But the one who intends to migrate from himself begins with death. How great are those men who have heeded this wondrous command and acted accordingly—"Die before you die."
>
> *Kavir,* p. 55

Everyone acquainted with Dr. Shari'ati knows well that not only is the study and reading of his works and thoughts instructive and rewarding, but also his way and method of life were the reflection of a correct and profound vision of the world, a ray emitted by his faith. Here, we will set forth only an outline, a sketch, of a life that consisted entirely of work, activity, faith, love and responsibility—the life of a conscious and dedicated man. We ask forgiveness of him and his friends for the inadequacy of our presentation.

Sketch of a Life

In truth, life itself was no problem for him, but only how to live and for what purpose. For this reason, from the very beginning of his life, he was not only concerned with the shaping of his life and imbuing it with meaning, but he also felt intensely the weight of the burden of the trust that he had inherited from his forefathers and ancestors. He wished to carry that burden to its destination as swiftly as possible, and as he recalled in his last letter, he never wasted a single moment or permitted it to pass without profit and result:

> By the grace of God Almighty, Whose miraculous love for me induces shame and pain in my heart and nearly causes my spirit to explode in its agitation, and without in any way being worthy of it, I have entered on such a path that I cannot permit myself to spend a single instant of my life on personal happiness. God's support of me compensates for my weaknesses, and what pleasure could be greater than this, that my life, destined to pass in any event, should pass in this fashion?
>
> From Shari'ati's last letter to his father

There weighed upon his life not only the burden of the trust he had inherited from his own ancestors and forefathers, but also the heavy burden of the search for truth and justice that has been borne throughout history and in every age by the oppressed, the humiliated and the afflicted, the burden of the trust made fully manifest by Husayn, the heir of Adam, the burden carried by Zaynab to the very court of Yazid in Damascus, the burden that everyday weighs more heavily on the shoulders of the men of God.

The form of solitude, exile, defeat, despair and pain was to be seen, in that desert covered with blood; it raised its head above the red wash of martyrdom, and stood silent and alone.

Husayn, the Heir of Adam, pp. 16-17

He believed that inheritance is a philosophical and credal fundamental of Islam by means of which Islam wishes to establish a purposive continuity running through the different events and occurences that have happened, are happening, and will happen in different times and places. They are linked together by means of this continuity; they are born and they die as the result of a logical causality and a scientific law; they succeed each other and influence each other; and each of them forms a link in a single continuous chain that extends from the beginning of humanity with Adam down to the end of the system of contradiction and struggle at the end of time. This logical continuity, this inevitable progression, is known as history.

This heavy burden of the trust of history, which he never forgot even for a moment, was transferred to him from his close ancestors and forefathers and illumined his whole life. His life began in the desert and ended with the attainment of a comprehensive historical and social ideology, a message for the intellectual guidance of the young generation, and the search for discovery of that "median path" that is the need of our times. Consciously and deliberately, he traversed the destined path of all those who felt and suffered, as he did, the pain of our age, and he became one more among the martyrs and witnesses of history—

A pure essence is fit to receive God's grace;
Not every rock and clod is turned to coral and pearl.

It is not fortuitous that like many great figures of science and religion, Shari'ati had his roots in the countryside. He was indeed proud of his ancestors, who were among the first-ranking religious scholars of their age, for choosing the isolation of the Kavir[2] in preference to the tumult and confusion of the city. Let us quote his own words:

> About eighty-five years ago, before the beginning of the Constitutional Revolution, my grandfather studied theology, philosophy and jurisprudence with his maternal uncle, Allama Bahmanabadi, and used to engage in philosophical debate with Hakim Asrar. Even though he was living in the remote and obscure village of Bahmanabad near Mazinan, his fame spread to the learned circles of Tehran, Mashhad, Isfahan, Bukhara and Najaf. In Tehran in particular he was renowned as a genius, and Nasir ad-Din Shah invited him to the capital. There he taught philosophy at the Sipahsalar madrasa, but the urge for solitude and isolation, strong in his blood, drew him back to his retreat in Bahmanabad. It was the time of maturity, when he could have had position and authority, assumed the leadership and direction of men, and enjoyed fame and influence. But he deliberately turned his back on it all.

Shari'ati derived much benefit from the life of his pure ancestors. He learned in particular "the philosophy of remaining a human being in an age when life is polluted, when remaining a human being is extremely difficult, and when a repeated jihad is needed everyday, and when jihad cannot be waged!"

> Akhund Hakim was my paternal grandfather. How delightful were the stories they would tell me of him! It is to these stories that I trace the origin of many of the deep and unconscious feelings that exist in the profundity of my soul . . . . It is almost as if I can see myself in him living fifty or eighty years ago . . . and I am grateful to him that he was as he was and that he acted as he acted.
>
> *Kavir*, pp. 9 ff

His paternal uncle was also one of the most outstanding pupils of the celebrated scholar Adib Nishapuri, but after studying jurisprudence, philosophy and literature, he followed the custom of his ancestors and returned to Mazinan.

Shari'ati regarded as his own the whole legacy of humanity and scholarship that his ancestors had left behind. He considered their spirit as living on in him and looked upon it as a guiding lamp, lighting his path.

---

[2] Kavir: the extensive desert that makes up almost two-thirds of the Iranian plateau. (TR.)

It was above all his father who was his spiritual teacher, in such a way that the son became a shining reflection of his father's essence.

> My father broke with tradition and did not return to the village after completing his studies. He stayed in the city, and strove mightily to preserve himself with knowledge, love and jihad in the midst of the swamp of urban life . . . . I am the result of his decision to stay, and the sole heir of all the estates and property he left behind in the domain of poverty . . . . I am the bearer of his cherished trust, laboring beneath its awesome weight . . . .
>
> *Kavir*, p. 19

Aqa Muhammad Taqi Shari'ati, the great teacher and mujahid and the founder of the "Center for the Propagation of Islamic Truth" in Mashhad, is one of the founders of the Islamic intellectual movement in Iran. He has continuously rendered brilliant service for forty years in the propagation of religion in a logical, scientific and progressive fashion. In particular, he has been in the forefront of efforts to bring the modern-educated youth back to faith and Islam, delivering them from materialism, worship of the West, and hostility to religion. "The idea of taking the Qur'an as the central means for teaching, studying and propagating the teachings of Islam and Shi'ism, and the creation of a special school of Qur'anic exegesis during the last few years, is largely his work" (Shari-'ati, *In Answer to Some Questions*, p. 162).

We emphasize the influence of his father upon Shari'ati because, as everyone will agree who knows this noble, dignified and scholarly man, this will help us to understand the different dimensions of Shari'ati's life. It will also confirm this truth, that when a person of genius and abundant intelligence is entrusted to a skilled teacher, to be educated under the proper conditions, he will be able to break the barriers of the commonplace, to outstrip his own age, and to become a source of influence instead of a recipient, active instead of passive. Those who are acquainted to some degree with the elder Shari'ati, and are aware of the different dimensions of his life—scholarly, religious, social, political and human—know of his devotion, his patience and ability to endure, his profound knowledge.

They know, too, his religious and philosophical writings, such as *Khilafa and Wilaya in Qur'an and Sunna, Revelation and Prophethood, Ali, Witness to the Message, The Promise of Religions, The Utility and Necessity of Religion, The Economics of Islam,* and, above all, his *Modern Tafsir (Tafsir-i Nuvin).* Finally, they are aware of his courageous struggles against all those elements which stifle and kill talent, even in universities and the religious environment, and his significant role in changing the methods of approach to Islamic questions, and in choosing a correct and suitable method for their examination in the convulsed age in which we live. In a time such as this, there are few such fathers and few such children.

> My father fashioned the first dimensions of my spirit. It was he who first taught me the art of thinking and the art of being human. As soon as my mother had weaned me, he gave me a taste for freedom, nobility, purity, steadfastness, faith, chastity of soul, and independence of heart. It was he who introduced me to his friends—his books; they were my constant and familiar companions from the earliest years of my schooling. I grew up and matured in his library, which was for him the whole of his life and his family. Many things that otherwise I would have had to learn much later, in adult life, in the course of long experience and at the cost of long-lasting effort and struggle, he gave to me as a gift in my childhood and early youth, simply and spontaneously. My father's library is now a world full of precious memories for me. I can remember each of his books, even their bindings. I love greatly that good, sacred room, which is for me the summation of my sweet, good, but distant past.
>
> *In Answer to Some Questions,* p. 89

But genius and talent break the limitations of every environment and outstrip their own age. In order to leave his mark, a man must regard existing fundaments simply as a point of departure for a creative leap forward, instead of permitting himself to be restricted and contained within his environment. Shari'ati was well aware of the restrictions of his environment, and the traditional forms that surrounded him, and he was determined to subject them to his own purposes instead of being subjected by them. In this, he was successful. He taught while still studying, and he developed intellectually in numerous ways so that everyone was aware he had already taken a few steps outside his environment and age.

Talent, a suitable environment, and above all, a belief in the veracity of the pure sources of Islamic truth, as well as a love and attachment for them, joined to intellectual and personal modesty in thought and behavior, enabled him to gain the utmost possible benefit from the possibilities that offered themselves to him, for the sake of his lofty aims. He described the general environment of his education as follows:

> What great blessings I have enjoyed in my life! I have failed to appreciate them adequately. No one has benefited from life as I have. The extraordinary, great, beautiful, passionate and creative spirits with whose path fate has caused mine briefly to cross, have in some measure taken up residence in my own frame. Even now I can clearly feel their presence within me, and I live through them and in them . . . .
>
> *Kavir*, p. 88[3]

Like the great spirits who were his teachers and preceptors, and those others who taught him meditation and jihad, and the various dimensions of true Islam, from whose abundant springs he gained inspiration and the love of truth, he too came to tread the paths of thought and reflection, of exertion and responsibility, of striving for perfection and eternity. But he never severed his ties with his first environment, and his family—and he never forgot the Kavir. Every mention of Mazinan he would preface with a smile of joy and contentment.

In his childhood and early youth, he appeared to be an ordinary student, one among countless others. Like the others, he went to school, took his examinations, and advanced from one year to the next, first of primary and then of intermediate education. At the same time, he was busy learning Arabic and the religious sciences. After he completed high school, out of love for the profession of teaching, he entered the teachers' training college—at that time, a reputable and important institution that prepared for the honorable profession of teaching

---

[3] *Kavir*, p. 88. Apart from his father, the first and greatest influence that he experienced, he mentions the following as having influenced him: Louis Massignon (the French orientalist), Muhammad Ali Furughi (Iranian scholar and politician), Jacques Berque (French Arabist and sociologist), and Gurwitsch (French sociologist). But these were all his teachers in a direct and familiar sense.

people who, for one reason or another, had been unable to enter the university. At the same time, he began his career as a writer with works such as the "Median School" (*Maktab-e Vasita*), on the philosophy of history. He also gave lectures to the students and intellectuals at the Center for the Propagation of Islamic Truth in Mashhad.

What fashioned him and determined the direction of his thought was not so much his conventional program of study, nor even the course of higher study that he followed abroad, as his love of learning and thought, and the creativity and commitment that he derived from his firm faith in the perspicuous religion of Islam, as well as from his earliest environment, which always remained a source of guidance for him. The Center for the Propagation of Islamic Truth in Mashhad, which for thirty years was the active and vital center of committed, intellectual Muslims in the city, contributed much to his formation; and in return, he played a great role in promoting its activities by delivering lectures, answering questions, and presiding over its sessions. From the outset, he was greatly interested in writing and lecturing as a means of intellectual development and deepening faith, and he was encouraged to pursue these interests by his eloquence and powerful, expressive pen. His knowledge of French and Arabic, even before entering the university, was at a level that permitted him to translate books from those languages. His translation of a book on Abu Dharr al-Ghaffari from Arabic, and a book on prayer from French, both souvenirs of his pre-university period, demonstrate the breadth of his thought and the scope of his work at this time. In addition, the eloquent and expressive introductions he wrote to the two translations, exemplify the direction and clarity of his Islamic thought in this period. In his view, Islam might be regarded as a "median school" among the different schools of philosophy, one intermediate between socialism and capitalism, which adopted the advantages and positive aspects of other schools of thought while avoiding their negative aspects.

He was chiefly concerned, however, with the ideological and anti-imperialist movements that at that time were sweeping across the Islamic world, from North Africa to Indonesia, and held out the promise of broad and comprehensive action. His translation of the book on Abu Dharr and the little but rich book on prayer, both products of this period of his life, drew his attention to the pure and unsullied sources of Islam, and exemplify his first interpretations of the life of the Prophet and the other leading figures of religion in the light of social concern. They both exercised an undeniable influence on the youth.

In 1956, the Faculty of Letters was founded in Mashhad, and Shari'ati became able to continue his studies while working as a teacher; he was, indeed, among the first students to be enrolled in the faculty. Here he had numerous clashes of opinion with his teachers, prompting him to develop further the line of thought he had chosen for himself. Even in the classes and lectures he attended, he played an active role, not being content to remain passive like the majority of students. Benefiting from this new opportunity for study, reflection, investigation and discussion, he developed a particular interest in the history of religion, the history of Islam and the philosophy of history. Many queries occurred to him in particular concerning Toynbee's philosophy of history, and he raised numerous objections to it.

His independence of thought and belief was demonstrated above all by his determined defense of truth and justice and the particular attention he paid to religious, social and political events that affected the destiny of the people. In the deathly silence that prevailed everywhere at that time,[4] he could never withdraw from the social struggles and conflicts, and the battle between truth and falsehood. With his speeches and his writings, and other resistance activities, he had caused the authorities to open a file on him. He was never able to remain silent and to accept the negative equilibrium that had been established in society. He fought on two fronts simultaneously. He opposed the extreme traditionalists who had spun a web around themselves, separated Islam from society, retreated into a corner of the mosque and the madrasa, and often reacted negatively to

---

[4] i.e., in the early years after the overthrow of Musaddiq in August 1953. (TR.)

any kind of intellectual movement within society; they had covered the brilliant truths of Islam with a dark veil behind which they themselves also hid. He also opposed the rootless and imitative intellectuals who had made the "new scholasticism" their stronghold. Both groups had severed their relations with society and the masses of the people, and humbly bowed their heads before the manifestations of corruption and decadence of the modern age.

At the University of Paris

The five years Shari'ati spent at the University of Paris provided him with the opportunity not only to continue his studies unimpeded by other concerns, but also to make the acquaintance of books generally unavailable in Iran (or, if available, often only in distorted form). He was able to examine and gain direct knowledge of different schools of social and philosophical thought and social behavior, as well as the works of philosophers, scholars and writers such as Bergson, Albert Camus, Sartre, Schwartz, sociologists such as Gurwitsch and Berque, and Islamologists such as Louis Massignon. He was particularly attracted to Islamic studies and sociology, and he studied these subjects formally. The analytical and critical school of French sociology left a considerable impression on him; but despite the attraction exerted on him for some time by this kind of sociology, his social vision was a compound of idea and action. He found unconvincing both the positivist approach to society, which regarded sociology as an absolute science, and the purely Marxist approach. Neither of these approaches was able to comprehend or analyze the realities of the non-industrialized world, the so-called "Third World." Shari'ati was constantly engaged in the search for a sociology that, irrespective of the status and development of capitalist society or the communist system, would be able to interpret and analyze the realities of the life of those peoples whose subjection to imperialism had been approved even by the communists of Europe, but who were struggling to gain their dignity and independence.

We know that part of Shari'ati's stay in France coincided with the tumultuous period of the Algerian revolution, a period in which different parties and groups in Europe, even scholars and sociologists, were adopting various positions, positive and negative, on the fate of a Muslim people who had been subjected to imperialism for more than a century and were engaged in a fierce jihad, a life-and-death struggle, carrying their battle into France itself. The position of the French Communist Party and the Algerian Communist Party, both of which supported the continued annexation of Algeria by France and opposed the Algerian revolution, was extremely instructive. Shari'ati devoted much attention and thought to what was taking place in Algeria, for he never considered himself separate from the anti-imperialist struggles of Muslim peoples and regarded himself a partner in their destinies. But the bloody revolution in Algeria belonged to another category, one all its own; it was something nobody could ignore, whether friend or enemy. The anti-imperialist struggle in Algeria had few if any precedents. It involved ten million Muslims—peasants, mountaineers, the whole Muslim population of the country—in a war against one of the most powerful armies of imperialism, and the French war machine that included 500,000 soldiers. The Algerian people produced a million martyrs, but finally cut off the enemy's line of retreat and brought it to its knees.

A factor of great significance was that all justice-loving Muslim forces, whether in the Arab world or beyond, supported the Algerian movement, regarded it as their own, and felt it in their own beings. At the instructions of the Algerian National Liberation Front, a large number of Muslim students, even those who were in their last years of study at the Faculty of Medicine and the Polytechnique, abandoned their studies and joined the ranks of the Algerian mujahidin, voluntarily filling all the different posts and functions required by the liberation struggle.

Another dimension of the struggle consisted of the theories and ideas that it produced: philosophical, sociological and psychological analyses designed to understand and explain the deep roots of the Algerian question. This theoretical activity,

which took place both inside the Algerian movement and outside of it, was reflected in numerous books and articles in
different languages. *El-Moudjahid*, the organ of the Algerian
Liberation Front, played a particularly prominent role, reflecting and analyzing the struggle in ideal form. French intellectuals also contributed much to this activity.

The essays and books of Franz Fanon drew particular attention. Originally from Martinique, he had taken Algerian
nationality, and he was a psychologist by profession. He joined
the ranks of the Algerian revolution at its very inception, and
produced numerous important works, such as *The Damned of
the Earth* and *The Fifth Year of the Algerian Revolution*.

Fanon was discovered and presented to the Europeans by
Jean-Paul Sartre. But he was first truly adequately discussed by
Dr. Shari'ati, in an article he wrote in 1962 for one of the
sociopolitical journals published by the Iranian students in
Europe. He regarded the book *The Damned of the Earth*, with
its profound sociological and psychological analyses of the
Algerian revolution, as a valuable intellectual gift to be presented to all those engaged in the struggle for change in Iran. By
expounding certain theories of Fanon, which previously had
been almost entirely unknown, and translating some of the
conclusions in his book, Shari'ati enabled the echo of Fanon's
thought and outlook to reach the Iranian popular movement of
which he was a part. Under the influence of Fanon, phrases
such as the following began to appear in his pronouncements:

> Come, friends, let us abandon Europe; let us cease this nauseating,
> apish imitation of Europe. Let us leave behind this Europe that always
> speaks of humanity, but destroys human beings wherever it finds them.

Thanks to the suitable presentation of his ideas by Shari'ati,
who fully sympathized with him and felt the truth of his statements in the very depth of his soul, Fanon became known and
appreciated in Iran, with the result that a number of discerning
people devoted themselves to further study and translation of
his work.

Shari'ati similarly played a great role in making known the
ideas of other African revolutionary writers, including Umar
Uzgan, author of *The Best of All Struggles (Afdal al-Jihad)*, as

well as a number of non-Muslim writers and poets. For he was convinced that the ideas that were taking shape in various popular and Islamic movements in Africa could inspire a new intellectual dynamism in the social and political struggles of the Iranian Muslims, and indeed, he always advised his friends and pupils to benefit intellectually from anything the genuine movements of Islamic struggle in our age have to offer.

His study of the works and ideas of committed thinkers and writers, while he was in Europe, as well as his personal encounter with some of them, did not affect him in a passive sense (as we see all too often with our intellectuals); rather, it inspired him to the development of new ideas, to orginality and creativity. He based his study and understanding of society not so much on formal and "official" sociology as on the actual and observable movements of society, and his objective studies and analyses were never devoid of criticism. Throughout the period of his residence and study in Paris—a period which ended in his receiving a doctorate in social sciences—he was engaged not so much in studying, memorizing and preparing for examinations, like other university students, as in developing himself as a mujahid, self-aware and discriminating.

There were three aspects of his activity that distinguished him from others at that time: intellectual struggle, practical struggle, and the struggle for the evolution of a true system of education. All three forms of struggle were oriented toward the people, or, more broadly conceived, to the umma. Instead of being totally absorbed by the tumult of student political activity, he sought to accomplish something for the sake of his people, something lasting and worthwhile. His writings and efforts were for the sake of his people, and he, more than anyone else, viewed the masses as his unique and irreplaceable point of orientation.

Shari'ati's residence in Paris coincided with a new and vital phase in the development of the progressive wing of the Iranian religious movement inside Iran. After a brief interval during which the breezes of freedom had blown over Iran, tyranny and repression reasserted their former place in the life of the country. Arrests and trials began again, long sentences of imprisonment were given, and barbaric torture was practiced. The chief target of the repression consisted of the religiously-oriented nationalists, especially those committed persons who had joined the Freedom Movement (*Nehzat-e Azadi*), the only group to come forward with a clear ideology and policy and a firm program of action. The glorious uprising of Muharram 12, 1383/June 5, 1963 also gave a new aspect to the Islamic movement in Iran, and separated the true mujahidin from the seasonal demonstrators.

Shari'ati belonged to this movement and considered it his own; hence he never desisted for an instant from writing and proclaiming the truth and analyzing the Islamic movement that had been shaped by the powerful leadership of Ayatullah Khumayni. At the same time, the majority of Persian-language publications appearing abroad had a non-religious or even anti-religious tone, even though the movement within Iran was fundamentally an Islamic one, and its whole basis was a progressive religious ideology. Iranian intellectuals abroad were overlooking the social realities of Iran and the true nature of the popular struggle, whether as a matter of evil intention, a conspiracy of silence, or the result of ignorance. They would relate only the briefest of details concerning events in Iran, conveying at the same time an implied criticism.

Fortunately, Shari'ati, together with a number of like-minded persons, was able to publish one of the most widely read Persian-language journals in Europe, and with his powerful intellect and pen, he made of it the most serious and realistic organ published in support of the popular movement. In this journal, a real harmony existed between the ideas of the intellectuals abroad and the nature of the struggle of the people within Iran.

In short, Shari'ati's period of study in France was marked by constant reflection and activity, and he came to embody one of the most influential currents of thought among Iranians abroad. Despite the significance of the various aspects of his activity, we cannot offer here a more detailed description of them, and must content ourselves with this brief indication of the influence exerted by the work of this militant thinker, Shari'ati.

Return to Iran

In an article published by *Kayhan*, one of the semi-official newspapers of Iran, on the occasion of the death of Shari'ati, we read as follows:

> In 1964, when Shari'ati deemed himself to be better equipped than ever before for the service of his country, his people and the perspicuous religion of Islam, he set out for Iran, with his wife and two children . . . . He was bearing with him a valuable gift for Iranian society. For he had discovered a whole new approach to religion, and it was his firm intention to wage a determined battle, with the weapon of logic and within the framework of true Islam, against the superstition, sectarianism, and hypocrisy that were harmful to nation and religion alike . . . . Upon returning to Iran, he was appointed professor at the University of Mashhad.

If we accept the first two statements quoted above, then the third would appear to be only logical and natural: if Shari'ati had brought such a valuable gift back to his country, it would have been entirely appropriate for him to be employed at a university. But this is not at all what happened. As soon as he arrived at Bazargan—the main Iranian border crossing from Turkey—after five years of absence from his country, he was arrested, in the presence of his wife and children, and immediately sent to prison. For a long time he was prevented from seeing his father. Even after being released from prison, he was obliged to work for many years as a teacher at various high schools and the College of Agriculture, at the same level he used to teach before going abroad; this, despite his doctorate and the "valuable gift for Iranian society" that he had brought. Such was the welcome given him by Iran. Throughout his life, his homeland was a prison for him where solitude, tribulation and all kinds of pressures bore down on him; but at the same time, this made him more determined to continue his struggle. After a number of years, without his seeking any appointment, he was appointed to the University of Mashhad, either by accident or by error. He then began to devote himself to the direct guidance of the young generation, and the students of different faculties all took great pride in calling themselves his students, according his lectures and classes an unprecedented welcome. But the university was displeased by this welcome; short-sightedness, pettiness, envy and malice combined to place obstacles in his path, and the University of Mashhad found itself unable to tolerate the existence of his classes. Shari'ati preferred free methods of teaching to conventional methods, and saw no distinction between freedom and knowledge. In any event, he was soon honored with forced retirement!

This retirement from the University of Mashhad gave him the opportunity to enter a new stage of intensive activity. By means of his lectures, free classes and analytical books written on social and religious topics, he created a new current of thought in the younger generation and in society as a whole. And the outcome of this was five hundred days in solitary confinement, without any trial, and finally martyrdom in exile!

Dr. Shari'ati was, in the fullest sense of the word, a committed believer in *tauhid,* an intellectual with an acute sense of social responsibility who never shirked his responsibility for a moment. In this age of ignorance, he demonstrated, together with a few other self-sacrificing souls, how it is still possible to give one's entire life—study, profession, work and even family —to the task of conveying the message. He devoted all of his time to jihad and to struggle, to the propagation of religion, in the hope that he might save this forgotten and unenlightened generation from its confusion and bewilderment. Despite the obstacles and difficulties, and the considerable attempts to sabotage his work made by corrupt elements cloaking themselves in piety, with his firm and forceful logic and rational mode of exposition, he left his mark on Iranian society, inflicting damaging blows on the ideological positions of domestic reaction and foreign imperialism. His numerous works are a guiding light for the younger generation. May his memory continue to be cherished!

His Works and Ideas

It is not so much the personality and activity of Shari'ati that are important as the works and ideas that he left behind, in the form of recorded lectures, class notes, books and numerous articles, that have been repeatedly printed or duplicated in editions of ten thousand copies or more. They have been sought out by the younger generation with such interest and eagerness that their profound impact can never be effaced from our memories or hearts. All that he said and wrote was expressed with the utmost sincerity, faith and conviction and bore testimony to an extraordinary creative capacity.

> Life and time no longer leave the pure and innocent alone and friendless. Their life will defend them and time will justify them. The impure can never pollute the innocent, however much they cast stones against them and loose their dogs upon them . . . .
>
> *Kavir*, p. 282

A glance at the fruitful, profound and original works of Dr. Shari'ati will show that he did not believe in oversimplified and superficial work. Yet, with his powerful pen and eloquent mode of expression, he was able to render comprehensible the most profound philosophical ideas and the most complex scientific and sociological topics; only the biased would dissent from this judgment. Some of his writings, however, appear to present difficulties: through his use of simile, metaphor and symbolic language, as well as by the concentrated meaning he injected into his words, doubts were aroused in the minds of people accustomed to thinking superficially. An opportunity for raising questions and objections was given to one-dimensional minds, whose constant habit it is to raise petty objections when confronted by searching and dynamic thought—in short, all those whose minds are sluggish and whose taste is perverted and who have forgotten the Qur'anic principle, "Dispute with them by the fairest of means" (Qur'an, 16:125).

Although the theories of Shari'ati have a religious orientation, they have a sound epistemological, philosophical, historical and sociological basis, and evolve from a constant dialectic of practice and reflection.

We can say that in the view of Shari'ati, correct thought is the prelude to correct knowledge, and correct knowledge is the prelude to belief; these three taken together are the necessary attributes of an aware conscience and of any movement that strives in practice and theory for the attainment of perfection. Superficial conviction and belief without awareness soon take on the form of fanaticism and superstition, and become obstacles in the path of social construction. Without ideological change, no profound change is possible in society, and it is precisely a profound ideological and intellectual change that is now needed more than anything else in the fast-moving, modern world. Such a change must originate in the depths of the being and consciousness of the individual before assuming the form of a general movement, in such a way that fixed and motionless forms that have become crystalized into ineffective "sacred" institutions should be transformed into moving and active elements, with a clearly defined role in the existential movement of society.

The correct knowledge of Islam is attainable on the basis of a philosophy of history grounded in *tauhid* and a "sociology of *shirk*," that sets forth the realities of society as they are. Shari-'ati's historical and symbolical analysis in *Husayn, the Heir of Adam* demonstrates that Islam is not a human ideology, pertaining to a particular time or place, but is like a stream, running through the entirety of human history, originating in remote mountain springs and traversing its rocky path before reaching the sea. This stream never ceases to flow, and at certain times, the Prophets and their successors come to quicken the force of its current. The whole of history is a struggle between truth and falsehood, a battle between monotheist and polytheist, a clash between oppressed and oppressor, between the deprived and the usurper. The form of this struggle and clash has been set forth symbolically in the story of Cain and Abel, as well as (in simpler form) in the struggle of the Prophet Moses, upon whom be peace, against the Pharaoh, Croesus and Balaam, who represent respectively opulence, power and deception in human history, as well as being all three *mushrik*.

The priesthood (*mala'*) and the opulent (*mutrif*) together comprise the exploiting classes that have always opposed the prophets, whereas the deprived, the oppressed and the pious have always stood with the prophets and the martyrs. Belief in *tauhid* is inseparable from the social and historical responsibility and commitments of those who profess it, so that the society that believes in *tauhid* is also a society that must practice jihad.

This eternal struggle begins in the very morning of man's social history, in the time of Adam, and the standardbearers in the battle for justice have always been the Prophets and the righteous. Thus the social movement of men has been joined to the world-view of *tauhid* and brought into harmony with it.

The burden of the trust of *tauhid* was entrusted in history, after the Prophet himself, peace and blessings be upon him, with the institution of the Imamate, with Ali and his descendants. But in the course of time, Shi'ism, which had begun as a protest by Ali, Husayn and Zaynab, became a tool in the hands of the possessors of money and might, and in the Safavid and post-Safavid periods, despite the guidance of the Imamate, its true visage became hidden beneath the dust of opportunism, vacillation, and misinterpretation, and the truth became lost. The following books and classnotes of Shari'ati may be referred to in this connection: *Husayn, the Heir of Adam, 'Ali: The School of Unity and Justice, Waiting for the Religion of Protest, Umma and Imamate, Alawi Shi'ism and Safavi Shi'ism, Abu Dharr al-Ghaffari, Salman-i Pak, Martyrdom, The Responsibility of Being Shi'a.* In them can be heard the re-echoing voice of Shari'ati in defense of the truth and true Islam, and together they represent the direction of Shari'ati's thought and the profound historical and religious analysis in which he engaged.

Another direction of Shari'ati's thought was the sociology of *shirk*, the realistic and critical analysis of present-day societies. Under this heading, he discussed the role of the different groups and strata of society; particularly the intellectuals, the competing ideologies and schools of thought existing in the world, and the role of different civilizations and cultures, all of them deprived of belief in *tauhid*. He finds that contemporary man, without *tauhid*, is in the last analysis an "alienated being, and that his science, once deprived of conscience, becomes a kind of neo-scholasticism, where pretenders take the place of true intellectuals." (See *The New Scholasticism, Civilization and Renewal, Alienated Man, The Sociology of Shirk, the Intellectual and His Responsibility, Existentialism and Nihilism,* etc.)

From the purely sociological point of view, we may say that few Iranian scholars have examined the reality of contemporary Islamic society in our age with the same penetrating realism as Shari'ati. What was important for him were not abstract concepts, but existing realities—values, modes of conduct, and the idea- and belief-structures prevailing in Islamic society.

In order to undertake such an analysis of society, Shari'ati did not think it adequate for intellectuals to be acquainted merely with European currents of thought on the one hand, and the social realities of their own society on the other. Such a limited knowledge might, in fact, lead them astray and suggest to them unrealistic conclusions. The analysis of existing realities is possible only through recourse to the terms, expressions and concepts that exist in our philosophy, culture, religion and literature, which are, in some cases, richer and more exact than their analogues in foreign languages. The translation and repetition of the stereotyped concepts of Western sociology, born of the analysis of nineteenth-century European industrial society and the aggressive, imperialist society of the first half of the twentieth century, can in no way be of value to us, for those concepts have nothing in common with our contemporary life. We must analyze the particular values and relations that have taken shape within our society and correspond to the specific nature of our social life, our psychic make-up and our modes of social behavior, as well as the existing realities in society and the psychological reactions of individuals to them. For this purpose, we must choose whatever has taken shape in the history of Islamic society in Iran and suggests a comprehensive system of sociological concepts and terms, and make our analysis on its basis. From this point of view, terms such as umma, imamate, justice, martyrdom, taqiya, taqlid, patience, unseen, intercession, migration, unbelief, *shirk, tauhid* and the like, are far more expressive than corresponding or similar European terms.

Shari'ati always placed his finger on the realities and avoided abstract thought. He was a realistic and committed sociologist who was enabled by his specifically Islamic mode of vision and thought to go beyond both positivist and Marxist sociology in the examination of his own society, and through the application of a profound historical and religious method, he endowed contemporary Islamic sociology with new dimensions. He carried out a realistic analysis and sociological criticism of both the "static" dimension of society—the present structure of conduct, value and beliefs of different groups, religious and non-religious—as well as the "dynamic" dimension, i.e., the historical changes and developments traversed by the Islamic umma and Iranian society in different eras. However, he did not accept the notion of "neutrality" in a science such as sociology, and could not accept that the sociologist should remain a pure observer of society, particularly in the present-day world where the concept of scientific neutrality has largely lost its meaning and social commitment and participation have taken the place of observation and description.

It is, therefore, appropriate to examine almost all the works and ideas of Shari'ati from a sociological viewpoint. He laid the foundations for a true and multi-faceted Islamic sociology, acting in this respect, too, as a pioneer.

What is important for us is that he examined history, the philosophy of history, religion and shari'a, and sociology, all within the framework of the general world-view of *tauhid*, so that *tauhid* became the intellectual and ideological foundation of both a philosophy of history, uncovering the past fate of man and human society, and a prediction of their future destinies.

All of his philosophical, historical and sociological analyses were joined, then, to a belief in *tauhid*, as he himself explains in the clearest fashion:

> *Tauhid* may be said to descend from the heavens to the earth, and leaving circles of philosophical, theological and scientific discussion, interpretation and debate, it enters the the affairs of society. It poses the various questions that are involved in social relationships—class relations, the orientation of individuals, relations between the individual and society, the various dimensions of the social structure, the social superstructure, social institutions, the family, politics, culture, economy, ownership, social ethics, the responsibilities of individuals and society. *Tauhid* thus provides the intellectual foundation for all the affairs of society.

This aspect of *tauhid* may be said in a general sense to constitute the ideological basis, the intellectual cement for the *tauhid*-oriented society—a society based on a material and economic structure exempt from contradiction and an intellectual and credal structure free of contradiction. The question of *tauhid* and *shirk* becomes, then, one relating to a universal philosophy of sociology, to the ethical structure of society and its legal and conventional systems.

This new approach that situated the idea of *tauhid* on the social plane and connected the understanding of society to the concept of *tauhid*, represents a stage beyond contradiction and opposition. Shari'ati's sociology was a reflection of his world-view, a world-view that brought practical results in society. He saw in the world of society a continual struggle between social *tauhid* and social *shirk*, a struggle that has lasted throughout history and that he analyzed in dynamic terms:

Just as the world-view of *tauhid* interprets existence in a unitary sense, so too it interprets human society in a unitary fashion. Just as on the plane of universal being *tauhid* is in opposition to diverse and contradictory forces, to the various deities of pagan pantheons, to the unseen and supernatural forces that are to influence men's destinies, and the processes of nature, so too *tauhid* in human society negates the terrestrial deities that impose themselves on men, usurping their powers and determining complex systems of society and social relationship among classes—in a word, it negates *shirk* on the human plane.

For Shari'ati, neither the Islam of the scholar nor the Islam of the common people was of value, but only the "Islam of the conscious and aware"; he preferred the intellectual and enlightened Muslim to both the scholar and the commoner. In Islam, the making of the self and the changing of the self presuppose and accompany each other; it is in this sense that the celebrated sentence—of which Shari'ati was so fond—is to be understood: "Life is conviction and struggle, and nothing more."

This is the vital and urgent message for the conscious Muslim of our age, a message he addressed particularly to the sincere and enlightened youth—"for once youth acquires conviction and faith, it will devote itself fully to them, and be swiftly transformed into an active element in the struggle for the realization of the goals of Islam."

The work of Shari'ati was of undeniable effect in this respect.

Bibliography

The late Dr. Shari'ati was a hard-working writer, a committed intellectual eager to convey his message, and at the same time, he possessed great genius and creativity. He always had something new to say or to write, so that it is not possible to present here all of his works and ideas. The only correct method for gaining an understanding of him is to refer directly to the writings that he left behind in the course of his brief but active life. The number of his lectures, discussions, answers to questions, sociological and historical analyses and writings, runs into the hundreds. Most of them have been frequently reprinted at home and abroad, in thousands of copies; taken together, they form a sort of "Encyclopedia of Islam." A glance at the titles of his works and lectures will show that he was always looking for new topics and subjects, and his mind never ceased its creative activity. His guiding light was the pure Islam of its first devoted adherents and the Qur'an. Despite the number of his writings, he seldom repeated any subject, and it is therefore necessary to refer to all that he wrote in order fully to appreciate his thought. Here we mention the titles of a few of his works accessible to us at the time of writing, in order to honor his memory—the memory of a brief life lived with firm faith that created a new current of thought among the educated youth, both in university and traditionalist circles.

May his soul rest in peace!

Abu Dharr Ghaffari, translation, Mashhad, 1335/1956.
Alawi Shi'ism and Safavi Shi'ism, lecture at Husayniya-yi Irshad.

Ali: A Truth Shrouded in Legend, lecture at Husayniya-yi Irshad.

Ali, the Perfect Man, lecture at Husayniya-yi Irshad.

Ali: The School of Unity and Justice, lecture printed by Husayniya-yi Irshad, Azar 1348/1969.

Allama Iqbal, congress in commemoration of Iqbal held at Husayniya-yi Irshad.

Appointment With Abraham, lecture given at the University of Mashhad on the philosophy of the hajj.

Approaches to the Understanding of Islam, lecture at Husayniya-yi Irshad, 1347/1968.

Approaches to the Understanding of Islam, second lecture at Husayniya-yi Irshad, 9 Aban 1347/1968.

Art in Expectation of the Promised One, lecture at the University of Mashhad.

Belief in Science, lecture at the University of Mashhad.

Civilization and Renewal, lecture given to the society of social science teachers of Khorasan.

Culture and Ideology, lecture at the Teachers' Training College, Tehran, printed by Husayniya-yi Irshad.

The Economic and Class Roots of the Renaissance, lecture at the Commercial High School.

Existentialism, lecture at the National University.

The Extraction and Refinement of Cultural Resources, lecture at the Petroleum College, Abadan.

Father, Mother, We Are Accused, lecture at Husayniya-yi Irshad.

Fatima the Unique, lecture on the role of woman in Islam, first given at Husayniya-yi Irshad, 1350/1971.

The First Blossoming of Islamic Spirituality in Iran, translated from the French of Louis Massignon.

The Four Prisons of Man, lecture given at Pedagogical High School.

"From Migration to Death," part of the book *Muhammad, Seal of the Prophets,* vol. I, published by Husayniya-yi Irshad.

From Where Shall We Begin? lecture given at Aryamehr University, printed by Husayniya-yi Irshad.

A General Syllabus of Islamology, 19 lessons, 1350/1971.

The History of Religions, duplicated at the Faculty of Letters, Mashhad.

Husayn, the Heir of Adam, lecture given at Husayniya-yi Irshad, Ashura 1349/1970.

If Ali Had Said Yes, lecture at Husayniya-yi Irshad.

In Answer to Some Questions and Criticisms, talk given at Husayniya-yi Irshad with the participation of Muhammad Taqi Shari'ati and Sadr Balaghi.

The Intellectual and His Responsibility, lecture at Husayniya-yi Irshad.

Islamology, vol. I, Mashhad, 1347/1968.

Kavir: History in the Form of Geography, Mashhad, 1349/1970.

Lessons in Tauhid, the History of Religions and Schools of Sociology, a collection of 25 lessons given at Husayniya-yi Irshad.

"Let Us Arise and Advance," lesson 20 of *Islamology,* 1350/1970.

The Machine in the Captivity of Machinism, lecture at Aryamehr University.

Man in Modern Civilization, lessons in the history of civilization given at the Faculty of Letters, Mashhad.

Man Without Self—Two Concepts of Alienation, published by Muslim Students Association of the Faculty of Letters, Tehran.

Martyrdom and Its Sequel, two lectures concerning Zaynab given at Husayniya-yi Irshad, Ashura 1351/1972.

The Median School, Mashhad, 1335/1956.

Methodology in the Sciences, lecture at the Commercial High School.

The Pain of Existence, lecture.

The Philosophy of History in the Abrahamic Religions, lecture at Husayniya-yi Irshad.

"The Philosophy of Scientific Determinism in History," lesson 25 of *Islamology,* Urdibihisht 1351/1972.

A Plan for the Study of Culture, lecture at the Petroleum College, Abadan.

Reasons For the Decline of Religions, lecture at the National University.

Religion Against Religion, lecture at Husayniya-yi Irshad.

Religion and Its Destiny, lessons given at the Faculty of Letters, Mashhad.

The Responsibility of Being Shi'i, lecture at Husayniya-yi Irshad, Aban 1350/1971.

The Revolutionary Role of Remembrance and the Reminders, Husayniya-yi Irshad, Shahrivar 1351/1972.

A Revolution in Values, lecture at the University of Tehran.

Science or the New Scholasticism, lecture at the Faculty of Medicine, Tehran.

The Sociology of Shirk, lecture at the Faculty of Letters, Tehran.

Specimens of Lofty Ethics, translation from the book of Kashif al-Ghita.

Supplication, translation, Mashhad, 1328/1948.

"Tauhid, a Philosophy of History," lesson 21 in the series *Islamology,* Husayniya-yi Irshad, Farvardin 1351/1972.

"Umma and Imamate," *Islamology,* vol. II, 1352/1973.

The Unjust, the Disobedient, the Faithless, Husayniya-yi Irshad, Aban 1351/1972.

Waiting for the Religion of Protest, lecture given at Husayniya-yi Irshad, 1350/1971.

What Shall Be Our Support? essay, Paris, 1961.

World-View, lecture at the Petroleum College, Abadan.

Yes, Thus It Was, O Brother, lecture at Husayniya-yi Irshad.

Note

Most of Dr. Shari'ati's lectures have been published in duplicated collections of up to 200 pages each. But since each sets out a particular concept and topic, I thought it better to mention each item separately without any attempt at classification.

There exist numerous unpublished and out-of-print works of Dr. Shari'ati, as well as numerous tape recordings of his lectures that unfortunately cannot be mentioned here. It will be necessary one day to draw up a complete bibliography of his work.

Gh. A.T.

A complete translation of Ravish-i Shinakht-i Islam, *comprising two lectures given at Husayniya-yi Irshad in Aban 1347/October 1968.*

Approaches to the Understanding of Islam

BEFORE I BEGIN discussing the subject itself, it may be appropriate to mention a number of points by way of introduction and reminder. These points may not be directly connected to my subject, but they have priority, insofar as they relate to fundamental and vital problems.

In recent years, most intellectuals have come to believe that talking is no longer of any use, and that to speak of our sufferings is of no benefit. Until now, we have constantly talked and discussed our sufferings without doing anything or undertaking any action. We must therefore close the era of talking, and everyone must begin acting by reforming his family or his city.

In my opinion, this view is based on an oversight, because in reality we have *not* talked up to now, we have *not* spoken of our sufferings, we have *not* closely and scientifically analyzed our sufferings. All we have done is to moan in our misery, and it is obvious that such moaning is of no value.

Up to now, we have not discussed our psychological and social problems at all correctly. Sometimes the false impression may arise that we have diagnosed our ills and must now set about curing them, but unfortunately it must be said that we have *not* diagnosed our ills.

Those who have set to work and experienced the difficulties, diversions and misfortunes that assail man in his practical strivings, realize and feel full well how little we have spoken concerning our sufferings, and how slight is our awareness of our sufferings, our corruption, our perversions!

Not only have we not spoken enough concerning our beliefs and religious and ideological outlook; we have not spoken at all on the subject.

How can we say that we have diagnosed our ills and spoken enough concerning them, and that now is the time for action? We are a religious society; the basis of our work must be religious; but we still do not know our religion.

By profession I am a teacher, and when my students ask me for books concerning certain topics, I am unable to answer them, for no books on those topics exist in the Persian language. This is truly shameful.

Our nation prides itself on having followed the Ja'fari school and Ali for centuries. From the very first century of Islam, when Iran entered the Islamic community and swiftly discarded its ancient religion in favor of Islam, it has followed the school of Ali, the companions of Ali and the government of Ali, whether òfficially as is now the case, or practically, with respect to sentiment and belief. But today when a student asks me what book he shold read concerning Ali, or the first persons who followed Ali and laid the foundations for the history of Shi'ism in the very first century of Islam through their extreme loyalty to Ali, I can give him no answer.

All I know of those persons is their names.

For a nation whose religion is the religion of Ali, it is extremely shameful not to have written a single worthwhile book concerning Ali and his companions.

It is. shameful that after fourteen centuries, Ali should be made known to us by a Christian, Georges Jourdaq, and that Abu Dharr should be presented to us by Jaudat as-Sahhar, one of our Sunni brothers.

Salman Farisi was the first Iranian to embrace Islam; he is a source of pride to the Aryan race and to all Iranians. He was a great man and a genius who followed the Prophet at the very beginning of his call, and then became so close to him as to be considered part of his family. The only book concerning this man—a source of pride to Iran from the national, scientific, religious and Shi'i viewpoints—has been written by a French-man;[1] in Persian, not even four pages exist concerning him.

I do not know how we can claim that the stage of analysis and discussion is at an end, and that now is the time to begin work! I do not wish to say that this is not a time for action and work, because speaking and acting, analyzing and applying, must always be joined together. This was the practice of the Pro-phet: he never divided life into two sections, the first consisting exclusively of talk and the second, exclusively of action. It is an extremely naive claim to make that "we have spoken enough and now is the time for action." All we have done is to moan and lament plentifully, and I am also convinced that lamenting in pain must be abandoned. Instead, we must speak concerning our sufferings, out of a sense of suffering, but also "scientifi-cally." The school of thought in which we believe must be the basis of our work, activity and thought. We must know what kind of man Ali was, and we must make the acquaintance of Abu Dharr and Salman and the veracious transmitters from the Prophet and Ali.

Unfortunately, no readable, worthwhile book exists in Per-sian concerning these sacred personages who are deserving of respect from a purely human viewpoint, quite apart from any religious considerations. If six books on the subject have appeared recently, they are all translations; we ourselves have not yet taken pen in hand.

Someone who knows the Qur'an well is known in this coun-try as "accomplished" (*fazil*), not as a "scholar" (*'alim*). The scholars enjoy a higher rank than the accomplished, who know about such subjects as the Qur'an, the history of Islam, and the life of the Prophet and his Companions; who interpret and explain the Qur'an and are skilled in such matters. These people are the second-class scholars of Islam! If this mode of thinking be true, even the Prophet, Ali and Abu Dharr must be regarded as "accomplished," not "learned."

It is for this reason that I am convinced that the greatest, most urgent and most vital task confronting us today is to speak—to

---

[1] The allusion is to Louis Massignon's *Salman Pak et les premices spirituelles de l'Islam iranien*, Paris, 1934. (TR.)

speak correctly, to speak out of a sense of suffering, yet at the same time precisely and scientifically, and thus to analyze what afflicts us. For all those who have set to work in our country and elsewhere in the Islamic world in the hope of accomplishing something have seen very little result for their efforts, or no result at all. The reason is that when they set to work, they did not know what needed to be done, and it is certain that as long as we do not know what we want, we will also not know what to do.

Our first task is, then, the knowledge of our religion and our school of thought. Yes, centuries after our historical adhesion to this great religion, we must still begin, unfortunately, with an attempt at knowing our religion.

As I said in our previous session, there are various ways of knowledge of Islam. One is the knowledge of Allah, and comparing Him with the objects of worship in other religions. Another is the knowledge of our book, the Qur'an, and comparing it with other heavenly books (or books that are said to be heavenly). Yet another is the knowledge of the personality of the Prophet of Islam and comparing him with the great reforming personalities that have existed throughout history. Finally, one more is the knowledge of the outstanding personalities of Islam and comparing them with the prominent figures of other religions and schools of thought.

The duty of today's intellectual is to recognize and know Islam as a school of thought that gives life to man, individual and society, and that is entrusted with the mission of the future guidance of mankind. He should regard this duty as an individual and personal one, and whatever be his field of study, he should cast a fresh glance at the religion of Islam and its great personages from the viewpoint of whatever may be his field of study. For Islam has so many different dimensions and varying aspects that everyone can discover a fresh and exact vantage point for viewing it within his field of study.

Since my field of study is the sociology of religion and the project is connected with my work, I have tried to codify a kind of sociology of religion based on Islam and drawing on the terminology of the Qur'an and Islamic literature. In the course of my work and research, I came to realize that there are many totally untouched topics that we have not even imagined existed. One of the facts I encountered in my study of Islam and the Qur'an was the existence of scientific theories of history and sociology peculiar to the custom and method of work of the Prophet. What is implied here is something different from taking the Qur'an, certain verses of the Qur'an, the philosophy and certain methods used by the Prophet, or the political, social, psychological and ethical system of life of the Prophet, and then analyzing them by means of contemporary science. We might, for example, try to understand the cosmological verses of the Qur'an with the help of physics, or to deduce the meaning of the historical and sociological verses of the Qur'an in the light of sociology. What I mean is something quite different; namely, that I extracted from the Qur'an a whole series of new topics and themes relating to history, sociology and the human sciences. The Qur'an itself, or Islam itself, was the source of the ideas. A philosophical theory and scheme of sociology and history opened themselves up before me, and when I later checked them against history and sociology, I found them to be fully correct.

There are several important topics in the human sciences that I discovered with the aid of the Qur'an that have not yet been discussed by these sciences. One is the topic of migration. In the book *Muhammad, Seal of the Prophets,* published by the Husayniya-yi Irshad, the topic is discussed only in its historical dimension; i.e., the movement of peoples from one point to another. From the tone in which the Qur'an discussed emigration and migrants, from the life of the Prophet and, in general, from the concept of migration held in early Islam, I came to realize that migration, despite what Muslims imagine, is not merely a historical event.

The understanding that Muslims have of the hijra is that a number of the Companions migrated from Mecca to Abyssinia and Medina on the orders of the Prophet. They imagine that migration has the general sense in history of the movement of a primitive or semi-civilized people from one place to another, as a result of geographical or political factors, and that for Muslims, migration represents simply an event that took place in the life of the Muslims and the Prophet of Islam. But from the tone in which migration is discussed in the Qur'an, I came to perceive that migration is a profound philosophical and social principle. Then, turning my attention to history, I realized that migration is an infinitely glorious principle, and that it constitutes a totally fresh topic, one by no means as simple as history and historians have made it out to be. Even the philosphers of history have not paid attention to the question of migration as it truly deserves, for migration has been the primary factor in the rise of civilization throughout history.

All the twenty-seven civilizations we know of in history have been born of a migration that preceded them; there is not even a single exception to this rule. The converse is also true, that there is no case on record in which a primitive tribe has become civilized and created an advanced culture without first moving from its homeland and migrating.

I deduced this topic, which is of great relevance to both history and sociology, from Islam and the tone in which the Qur'an discusses migration and commands permanent and general migration.

All the civilizations in the world—from the most recent, the civilization of America, to the most ancient that we know of, the civilization of Sumer—came into being on the heels of a migration. In each case, a primitive people remained primitive as long as it stayed in its own land, and attained civilization after undertaking a migration and establishing itself in a new land. All civilizations are, then, born of the migrations of primitive peoples.

There are numerous subjects and topics that I came to understand in this way. Islam and the Qur'an, in proportion to my own degree of knowledge of them, helped me to understand questions of history and sociology in a better, fresher and more precise fashion. I thus came to realize that through applying the special terms of the Qur'an, it is possible to discover numerous topics even in the most modern of sciences, the human sciences.

The subject I now wish to discuss, with respect to the sociology of Islam, is the greatest dilemma of both sociology and history: the search for the basic factor in the change and development of societies. What is the basic factor that causes a society suddenly to change and develop, or suddenly to decay and decline? The factor that sometimes causes a society to make a positive leap forward; to change totally its character, its spirit, its aim and its form, in the course of one or two centuries; and to change completely the individual and social relationships obtaining in it?

Attempts to find an answer to this question have been continuing for centuries, and particularly during the last 110 years, all the different schools of sociology and history have constantly lavished clear and exact attention on the search for an answer. The question constantly raised is this: what is the motor of history, the basic factor in human society's development and change?

The various schools of sociology part company at this point, each one devoting attention to a particular factor.

Certain schools do not believe at all in history, but regard it as nothing more than a worthless collection of narrations from the past. They also refuse to accept that sociology should have any fixed laws, principles or criteria.

A certain kind of scientific anarchism exists in the world. It is pessimistic with regard to the philosophy of sociology and the human sciences, and considers accident to be the basic factor. It says that the changes, advancements, declines, and revolutions that take place in nations all come into existence as the result of accident. For example, suddenly the Arabs attacked Iran; by chance, Iran was defeated and later the Iranians became Muslim. By chance, Chengiz Khan attacked Iran; it so happened that Iran's government was weak at that time, so that it was defeated. The Mongols entered Iran, so that the Mongol culture and way of life became intermingled with the Irano-Islamic way of life, and a certain change took place. Similarly, the First and Second World Wars also broke out by accident; it was possible that they should not have taken place. In short, this school regards everything as the outcome of chance.

Another group is composed of the materialists and those who believe in historical determinism. They believe that history and society, from the very beginning down to the present, are like a tree, devoid of any volition. In its origin it was a seed. Then it emerged from the seed, appeared above the ground, put forth roots, stems, branches and leaves and grew into a great tree, compelled to yield fruit, to wither in winter, to blossom again in spring, to attain perfection and finally to decay. This group believes that human societies traverse a long life throughout history in accordance with determining factors and laws that play in human society exactly the same role as the laws of nature in the natural realm.

According to this belief, individuals can have no effect on the fate of their societies, and society is a natural phenomenon that develops according to natural factors and laws.

The third group consists of those who worship heroes and personalities. It includes the fascists and Nazis, as well as great scholars like Carlyle, who also wrote a biography of the Prophet of Islam, and Emerson, and the like. This group believes that laws are no more than a tool in the hands of powerful individuals and have of themselves no effect on society. Average and sub-average persons, equally, have no share in the changing of society; they too are like tools for others to use. The only fundamental factor in the reform or advancement of society, or the cause of its downfall, is the powerful personality.

Emerson says: "Give me the names of ten powerful personalities, and I will tell you the whole of human history, without ever studying it. Tell me about the Prophet of Islam, and I will tell you about the whole history of Islam. Present me with Napoleon, and I will expound for you the whole history of modern Europe."

In the view of this group, the destiny of society and mankind is in the hands of powerful personalities, who act as the guides for all societies. The happiness or wretchedness of societies does not, then, depend on the masses of the people, nor is it caused by inevitable laws of environment and society, nor is it the result of mere accident; it depends solely on great personalities who every now and then appear in societies in order to change the destiny of their own societies, and sometimes that of mankind.

In his biography of the Prophet of Islam, Carlyle writes as follows: "When the Prophet of Islam first directed his preaching to his own relatives, they all rejected him. It was only Ali, at that time a ten year-old boy, who arose in response to the call of the Prophet and gave him his allegiance." Carlyle then concludes, in the light of his own way of thought: "That small hand was joined to the large hand, and changed the course of history."

The opinion also exists that the people, the generality of society, do play a role in determining their destiny; but no school of thought, not even democracy in its ancient or modern forms, claims that the masses are the fundamental factor in social development and change. Democratic schools of thought believe that the best form of government is that in which the people participate; but from the time of Athenian democracy down to the present, none of these schools has believed that the broad masses of the people are the decisive factor in social change and development. The most democratic of sociologists, then, even while believing that the best form of government and of administrative and social organization is that in which the people participate by casting their votes and electing the government, do not regard the "people" as the basic factor of social change and development. Instead, they regard determinism, great personalities, the elite, mere chance or divine will as the decisive factor.

The worshippers of personality can be divided into two groups.

The first group consists of those who believe that a great personality like the Buddha, Moses or Jesus appears and changes human society. They are the pure hero-worshippers.

The other group consists of those who believe that initially a personality appears and then he is joined by a group of the elite, the outstanding geniuses of his people, so that a team comes into being. It is this elite team which directs society on a path and to a goal of its own choosing. This group might more correctly be called "elite-worshippers."

In Islam and the Qur'an, none of the foregoing theories is to be found. Now from the point of view of Islam, the prophet is the greatest of all personalities; and if Islam were to believe in the role of the prophet as the fundamental factor in social change and development, it would have to recognize all the prophets, and especially the Prophet Muhammad, as constituting that fundamental factor. We see, however, that this is not the case. The mission and the characteristics of the Prophet are clearly set forth in the Qur'an, and they consist of the conveying of a message. He is responsible for conveying a message; he is a warner and a bearer of glad tidings. And when the Prophet is disturbed by the fact that the people do not respond and he cannot guide them as he would wish, God repeatedly explains to him that his mission consists only of conveying the message, of inspiring fear in men and giving them glad tidings, of showing them the path; he is not in any way responsible for their decline or advancement, for it is the people themselves who are responsible.

In the Qur'an, the Prophet is not recognized as the active cause of fundamental change and development in human history. He is depicted rather as the bearer of a message whose duty it is to show men the school and path of the truth. His mission is then completed, and men are free either to choose the truth or to reject it, either to be guided or to be misguided.

"Accident" also has no decisive role to play in Islam, for all things are in the hand of God, so that accident, in the sense of an event coming into being without any cause or ultimate purpose, is inconceivable, whether in nature or in human society.

If personalities are mentioned in the Qur'an, other than the prophets, their mention is frequently joined with a sense of condemnation or distaste. Even if they are mentioned for their righteousness and purity, the Qur'an never considers them as an effective factor in their societies.

The conclusion we deduce from the text of the Qur'an is, then, that Islam does not consider the fundamental factor in social change and development to be personality, or accident, or overwhelming and immutable laws.

In general, those addressed by every school of thought, every religion, every prophet, also constitute the fundamental and effective factor of social change within that school. It is for this reason that we see throughout the Qur'an address being made to *al-nas*, i.e., the people. The Prophet is sent to *al-nas;* he addresses himself to *al-nas;* it is *al-nas* who are accountable for their deeds; *al-nas* are the basic factor in decline—in short, the whole responsibility for society and history is borne by *al-nas*.

The word *al-nas* is an extremely valuable one, for which there exist a number of equivalents and synonyms. But the only word that resembles it, structurally and phonetically, is the word "mass."

In sociology, the masses comprise the whole people taken together as an entity without concern for class distinctions that exist among them or distinguishing properties that set one group apart from another. "Mass" means, therefore, the people as such, without any particular class or social form.

Al-nas has exactly the same meaning, i.e., the masses of the people; it has no additional meaning. The words *insan* and *bashar* also refer to man, but they refer to ethical and animal properties respectively.

From this we deduce the following conclusion: Islam is the first school of social thought that recognizes the masses as the basis, the fundamental and conscious factor in determining history and society—not the elect as Nietzsche thought, not the aristocracy and nobility as Plato claimed, not great personalities as Carlyle and Emerson believed, not those of pure blood as Alexis Carrel imagined, not the priests or the intellectuals, but the masses.

We can fully realize the value of this point of Islamic doctrine only when we compare it with other schools of thought.

To whom do the various other schools of thought address themselves? Some of them address themselves to the educated and intellectual class; others, to a certain selected group within society. One addresses itself to a superior race, another to supermen, while yet another focuses its attention on a certain class of society, such as the proletariat or the bourgeoisie.

None of the privileges and distinctions assumed by these schools exists in Islam. The only fundamental factor in social change and development is the people, without any particular form of racial or class privilege, or any other distinguishing characteristics.

The following can also be deduced from the Qur'an: while the people are those to whom the Qur'an addresses itself and they constitute the axis and fundamental factor in social development and change, and while they are responsible before God, at the same time personality, chance and tradition also have been recognized as capable of affecting the destiny of society. According to Islam, there are then four fundamental factors of social development and change—personality, tradition, accident and *al-nas*, "the people."

Tradition, in the form derived from Islam and the Qur'an, has the sense that each society has a fixed basis, or in the words of the Qur'an, it has a road, a path, a particular character. All societies contain definite and immutable laws within themselves. A society is like a living being; like all organisms, it has scientifically demonstrable and immutable laws. From a certain point of view, then, all developments and changes that take place in a society take place on the basis of a fixed tradition and immutable laws that are the very fundament of social life.

Islam thus appears to approach the theory of determinism in history and society; but it has something further to say on the subject, modifying the law it has established. In Islam, we have both human society (*al-nas*) being responsible for its fate, and also the individuals that compose society being responsible for their destinies. The Qur'anic verses, "For them shall be what they have earned, and for you shall be what you have earned," (2:134) and "Verily God does not change the state of a people until they change the state of their own selves" (13:11) bear the meaning of social responsibility. By contrast, the verse, "Every soul is accountable for what it has earned" (74:38) sets forth the responsibility of the individual. Both society and the individual are therefore answerable for their deeds before the Creator, and each constructs his own destiny with his own hands.

In sociology, these two principles are apparently contradictory—on one side, the responsibility and freedom of man in changing and developing his society; on the other side, the notion of a determining, fixed, scientifically established law, one inaccessible to human intervention, and providing the immutable basis for the movement of society. But the Qur'an looks upon these two poles—the existence in society of determining, fixed and immutable laws, and the collective and individual responsibility of man for social change and development—in such a way that not only are they not contradictory, they even complement each other.

In nature matters lie similarly. An agricultural engineer has the responsibility of cultivating the trees and plants in an orchard, the responsibility of ensuring that they bear the best possible fruit, the responsibility of trimming and irrigating the plants and the trees. In all of these matters he has freedom of choice, and therefore also responsibility. But at the same time, we see that certain laws exist in botany, and it is on the basis of these determining and immutable laws that change and development take place in plants and trees.

In accordance, then, with his degree of knowledge and information, man can make use of the laws inherent in the plant, laws which are in themselves unchanging. An agricultural engineer can never establish new laws of botany, nor can he abolish any of the existing laws of botany. Those laws, pre-existent in nature, impose themselves ineluctably upon the agricultural engineer. But while he cannot change them, he does have the ability to manipulate the fixed practices and laws of botany by means of scientific intervention, and thus to benefit from the existing laws which he cannot change. On the basis of a new form, one lying fully within the scope of the existing laws, he can transform an inferior or average fruit into a superior one.

The responsibility of man in society is exactly similar. Society, just like the orchard, has been established on the basis of God-given norms and patterns, and its development and evolution is also founded on them. But at the same time man is responsible, and he cannot divest himself of his responsibility through reliance upon Khayyamian fatalism or historical determinism, thus ridding himself of accountability for the destiny of his society. For while stating that society is indeed founded upon immutable laws, the Qur'an does not deny human responsibility. According to the school of thought that the Qur'an represents, man has the responsibility of correctly recognizing the norms of society and of improving those norms for the advancement of his society. By what means should he do this? By means of his own knowledge.

Why is an agricultural engineer more responsible than others for the cultivation of an orchard and for increasing its yield? Because he is better informed concerning the norms of the orchard and as a result, enjoys greater freedom in changing the destiny of the trees and its plants. Similarly, the greater a man's knowledge of the norms that predominate in society, the greater is his responsibility for changing and developing society, and the greater, too, his freedom in doing so.

Islam, as a scientific school of sociology, believes that social change and development cannot be based on accident, for society is a living organism, possessed of immutable and scientifically demonstrable norms. Further, man possesses liberty and free will, so that by intervening in the operation of the norms of society, once he has learned of them, and by manipulating them, he may plan and lay the foundations for a better future for both the individual and society.

Thus on the one hand there exists the responsibility of man; and on the other hand, the belief that society, like a living organism, is founded on immutable and scientifically demonstrable laws.

Maybe this constitutes one of the meanings, from the viewpoint of sociology, of the well-known saying, "Neither determinism nor absolute free will, rather a position intermediate between them."[2]

We have, then, on the one hand, man, equivalent to will, and on the other, society, equivalent to norm. Norm (*sunnat*), in its Qur'anic usage is something unchanging, and man is directly responsible for his individual and social life; the combination of these two represents the "median position." Man is free in his deeds and actions—not determined—but obliged to follow the pre-existent laws of nature in order to realize his freedom.

---

[2] A dictum attributed to Imam Jafar as-Sadiq, indicating that the opposing poles of absolute determinism and absolute free will may be reconciled by the truth that lies between them. (Tr.)

"Personality" is not in itself a creative factor in Islam. Even the prophets are not regarded as persons who have created new norms in the existing society. From the point of view of sociology, the superiority of the prophets to other teachers—apart from the rank of prophethood itself—is that they have recognized the divine norms that exist in nature and the world better than mere reformers, and on this basis they have been better able to make use of their freedom as men to advance their aims in society. It is a truth fully attested by history that the prophets have always been more successful than reformers who were not prophets.

Reformers sometimes set out the best of theses and principles in their books, but they have never been able to change society or to create a civilization. The prophets, by contrast, have built new societies, civilizations and histories. It is not that they have established new norms in opposition to divine law—as the fascists and hero-worshippers might say—but rather, through the power of prophethood and extraordinary talent, they have discovered the divine norms existing in society and nature, and through the exercise of their will in conformity with these norms, they have performed their mission and attained their goal.

Accident also cannot exist in Islam in the philosophical sense of the word, for God intervenes directly and continuously in all affairs. Moreover, since accident has no logical cause or ultimate purpose, it cannot appear in society, nature or life.

However, a certain form of accident, understood in a particular sense, does exist in human fate. For example, Chengiz Khan appears in Mongolia, comes to power in accordance with social norms, and assembles a large force around him. But the defeat of Iran at the hands of Chengiz Khan is an accident; it was quite possible for it not to have occurred. Accidents of this type may very well affect the destinies of certain societies.

In short, four factors affect the destiny of societies—personality, accident, norm and people (*al-nas*). Among them the two most important are *al-nas* and norm, because *al-nas* represents the will of the mass of the people, and norm, the scientifically demonstrable laws existent in society.

Personalities in Islam are those who understand well the divine norms; who have discovered these norms by means of a scripture (in the particular sense accorded to scripture by Islam, that of wisdom and guidance), and make of this the secret of their success.

The proportional influence of each of these four factors on a given society depends on the circumstances of that society. In societies where *al-nas,* the mass of the people, are advanced and stand at a high level of education and culture, the role of personalities is reduced; but in societies that have not reached that level of civilization, for example a tribe or a clan, the personality or the leader may be influential. At each different stage of society, with respect to progress or backwardness, one of the four factors mentioned will have more effect than the other three.

In Islam, the personality of the Prophet had a fundamental and constructive role in bringing about change, development and progress, in building a future civilization and in changing the course of history. This was because he appeared in a particular geographical location—the Arabian peninsula—which, from the point of view of civilization, was just like its geographical position. That is, it was a peninsula surrounded on three sides by seas, but thirsting and deprived of water. It was a neighbor to the great civilizations of history: to the north, the civilization of Greece and Byzantium; to the east, the civilization of Iran; to the southeast, the civilization of India; to the northwest, the Aramaic-Hebrew civilization. It was also a neighbor to the religions of Moses, Jesus and Zoroaster, as well as to the totality of Aryan and Semitic civilizations. At the time of the appearance of the Prophet of Islam, all the civilizations in existence were gathered around the Arabian peninsula. But the peculiar geographical location of the peninsula decreed that just as none of the vapors that arose over the oceans ever reached the peninsula, so too not a trace of the surrounding civilizations ever penetrated the peninsula. The Prophet of Islam thus appeared in such circumstances that his personality was—from the point of view of a sociologist—the greatest factor in the change and development of society and history. Similarly, a historian looking at the great event that occured in the Arabian peninsula in the seventh (Christian) century will see that it absorbed into itself everything that surrounded it and laid the foundations for a great civilization and a lofty new society. When the historian then studies the peninsula and finds it an absolute vacuum from the point of of culture and civilization, with its people existing at the lowest level, he is bound to attribute all these signs of change and development, this most fundamental and greatest revolution in history, to the personality of Muhammad the son of Abdullah. The personality of the Prophet thus has a particular, indeed exceptional, status.

In general there are five major factors that build a man. First, his mother makes the structure and dimensions of his spiritual form. The Jesuits say, "Give me your child until he is seven years old, and he will remain a Jesuit until the end of his life, wherever he goes." The mother rears the spirit of man as something tender and sensitive, full of emotion, and gives each child its first instruction with her own gestures while suckling it.

The second factor in the making of man is his father, who makes the other dimensions of the spirit of the child after the mother.

The third factor that builds the outer and apparent dimensions of man is school.

The fourth is society and environment. The stronger and more powerful the environment, the greater will be its educative effect upon man. For example, if somebody lives in a village, the formative effect upon him of his environment will be less than in the case of one who lives in an extremely large city.

The fifth educative factor in the building of personality consists of the general culture of society or that of the world as a whole.

There are thus five dimensions which taken together form a mold into which the spirit of man is poured and from which it is extracted once shaped.

Education consists of the particular shape deliberately given to human spirits for the attainment of certain purposes. For if man be left to his own devices, he will develop in such a manner as to be unfit for the purposes of social life. We therefore provide men with certain molds within which to grow and develop according to our desires and the demands of the age.

But in the life of the Prophet of Islam, whose personality must be regarded as the greatest factor in historical change, none of the factors mentioned above affected his spirit. It was, on the contrary, the deliberate purpose of God that no mold or form should be imposed on his spirit, and no artificial or inculcated form should touch his soul, in the way that earns men the approval of their time and their environment. For that great man came precisely in order to break all molds, and if he had grown up within one of them, he would never have been able to complete his mission. For example, he might have become a great physician, but only according to Greek models; he might have become a great philosopher, but only according to Persian models; he might have become a great mathematician or poet, but only according to the models approved by his age. However, he was sent to grow and develop in an environment that was empty of culture and civilization, and to remain untouched by the influence of any of the five factors mentioned above.

It is for this reason that when the Prophet opens his eyes, he does not see his father. Even though he has his mother, the hand that would keep him free of all forms and molds draws him into the desert while his mother is still alive. It was then the practice of the Arabs to send their infants into the desert until they were two years of age, so that they would spend their infancy in the desert. They would then return to the cities to grow up in the care of their mothers.

By contrast with this practice, the Prophet Muhammad went back to the desert after returning to Mecca, and he stayed there until he was five. After some time his mother died. These wise and subtle divine measures preserved from the influence of all forms and molds the infant that was destined to shatter all existing molds—Greek, Eastern, Western, Jewish, Christian, Zoroastrian—and to create a new mold. Then again the hand of providence and fate removed him from the city to the desert in his youth, on the pretext of making him a herdsman, so that the urban environment might not impose its own approved forms on the spirit that had to develop in freedom. In order that society and the age might not leave any effect on the Prophet, he was, moreover, created in a society that had no general culture. In addition, he was unlettered—that is, he was unable to read or to write—because it was necessary that the mold of schooling also should not be imposed on him.

We see then that the greatest distinction and advantage enjoyed by the person who was to undertake such a mission lay precisely in his exemption from all forms and molds accepted in his age, all the forms that fashion man according to a stereotype. For the man who was destined both to destroy all fire temples and to close down all academies and establish in their place the mosque, the man who was destined to destroy all racial, national and regional forms and molds, should not himself be subject to the influence of any such form.

First, his father was taken from him so that his dimensions would not be imposed on the spirit of the Prophet. Then his mother was kept at a distance from him so that her maternal affection and tenderness should not taint with lyrical softness a spirit that had to be stern and powerful. He was, moreover, born in a dry peninsula, far removed from universal culture, so that his great spirit might not be affected by the educative influence of any culture, civilization or religion, for a spirit destined to endure and perform an extraordinary mission cannot be fashioned in any ordinary form. This apparent deprivation was in reality the greatest of advantages and distinctions for the person who was entrusted with the greatest role in the greatest event of history.

Second Lecture

My topic concerns different approaches to the knowledge and understanding of Islam. "Different approaches" constitutes a precise and important scientific concept, and it denotes methodology for the understanding of Islam.

The question of methodology is of extreme importance in history, and particularly in the history of science. The correct cognitive method for the discovery of truth is more important than philosophy, science or the possession of mere talent.

We know that in the Middle Ages, Europe spent a millenium in the most appalling stagnation and apathy, and that immediately after the end of this period, the stagnation and apathy gave way to a multi-faceted and revolutionary awakening in science, art, literature, and all areas of human and social concern. This sudden revolution and burst of energy in human thought resulted in the birth of the civilization and culture of today's world. We must now ask ourselves, "Why did Europe stagnate for a thousand years, and what happened to cause a sudden change in direction, so that in the course of three centuries, it discovered truths it had failed to perceive in a whole millenium?"

This is an extremely important question; it may, indeed, be the greatest and most important question that science must answer.

Without doubt, numerous factors caused the stagnation of Europe in the Middle Ages, and various causes suddenly awakened Europe from its sleep, setting it on the course of swift and dazzling progress in every respect.

We must point out here that the fundamental factor in the stagnation of thought, civilization and culture that lasted for a millenium in medieval Europe was the Aristotelian method of analogical reasoning. When this way of looking at questions and objects changed, science, society and the world also changed, and as a result of that, human life too. We are concerned here with culture, with thought and the scientific movement, and it is for this reason that we regard the change in methodology as the fundamental factor in the Renaissance. At the same time, it is true from the sociological point of view that the main factor in this change was the transformation of the feudal system into that of the bourgeoisie; this was caused, in turn, by the breaching of the wall that separated the Islamic East from the Christian West, the breaching brought about by the Crusades.

Method is then of far-reaching importance in determining progress or decline. It is the method of investigation, not the mere existence or non-existence of genius, that brings about stagnation and apathy or motion and progress. For example, in the fourth and fifth centuries before Christ, numerous great geniuses existed who cannot be compared with the geniuses of the fourteenth, fifteenth and sixteenth centuries. Aristotle was without doubt a greater genius than Francis Bacon, and Plato a greater genius than Roger Bacon. But what enabled the two Bacons to become factors in the advancement of science, despite their inferiority in genius to men like Plato, while those geniuses caused the millenial stagnation of medieval Europe? In other words, why should a genius cause stagnation in the world, and an average man bring about scientific progress and popular awakening? Because the latter has discovered the correct method of reasoning, by means of which even a mediocre intellect can discover the truth, while the great genius, if he does not know the correct method of looking at things and reflecting on problems, will be unable to make use of his genius.

It is for this reason that we see in the history of Greek civilization tens of geniuses gathered in a single place in the fourth and fifth centuries. The history of mankind has remained under their influence down to the present. But the whole of Athens was unable to invent a wheel, whereas in modern Europe, an average technician who cannot even understand the writings of Aristotle and his pupils has made hundreds of inventions.

The best example of this is provided by Edison, whose general perception was inferior to that of the third-class pupils of Aristotle, but who at the same time contributed more to the discovery of nature and the creation of industry than all the geniuses who have been trained in the Aristotelian school during the past 2,400 years. He made more than a thousand inventions, great and small. Thinking correctly is like walking. A person lame in one foot and unable to walk fast, if he chooses the right path, will reach his destination sooner than the champion runner who takes a rocky and winding path. However fast the champion may run, he will arrive late at his destination, if he reaches it at all; whereas the lame person who chooses the right route will attain his destination and goal.

The choice of correct method is the first matter to be considered in all the different branches of knowledge—literary, social, artistic and psychological. The first task of any researcher must therefore be the choice of the best method of research and investigation.

We must make full use of the experiences of history, and we must consider ourselves obliged, as the followers of a great religion, to learn and know Islam correctly and methodically.

Today is no time for the worship of what we do not know. The educated, in particular, have a heavier responsibility for acquiring knowledge of what is sacred to them; this is not merely an Islamic duty, but also a scientific and a human one. A person's character may be judged in accordance with his degree of knowledge concerning his beliefs, for the mere holding of a belief is no virtue in itself. If we believe in something that we do not fully know, it has little value. It is the precise knowledge of that in which we believe that may be counted a virtue. Since we believe in Islam, we must acquire correct knowledge of it and choose the correct method for gaining that knowledge.

The question now arises, what is that correct method? In order to learn and know Islam, we must not imitate and make use of European methods—the naturalistic, psychological or sociological methods. We must be innovative in the choice of method. We must of course learn the scientific methods of Europe, but we do not necessarily need to follow them.

Today, scientific methods have changed in all branches of knowledge, and new approaches have been discovered. In the investigation of religion as well, new paths must be followed and a new method must be chosen.

It is obvious that a single, unique method cannot be chosen for the study of Islam, since Islam is not a one-dimensional religion. Islam is not a religion based solely on the mystic intuition of man and restricted to the relationship between man and God; this is merely one dimension of the religion of Islam. In order to study this dimension, a philosophical method must be followed, because man's relation to God is discussed in philosophy, in the sense of general and unfettered metaphysical thought. Another dimension of this religion is the question of man's life on this earth. In order to study this dimension, use must be made of the methods that have been established in the human sciences of today. Then, too, Islam is a religion that has built a society and a civilization; in order to study these, the methods of history and sociology must be used.

If we look at Islam from only one vantage point, we will have seen only one dimension of this multi-faceted phenomenon; even if we see it correctly, this will not suffice for a knowledge of the whole. The Qur'an itself is a proof of this. It is a book that has many dimensions, some of which have been studied by great scholars throughout history. For example, one dimension comprises the linguistic and literary aspects of the Qur'an; the literary scholars have examined these minutely. Another dimension comprises the philosophical and credal themes of the Qur'an that the philosophers and theologians of today would do well to reflect upon. A further dimension of the Qur'an, one which has remained more obscure than all the others, is its human dimension, comprising historical, sociological and psychological matters. The reason for this dimension's remaining unknown is that sociology, psychology and the human sciences are far more recent than the natural sciences. Similarly, the science of history is the most recent science to have appeared in the world; it is something different from historical data or the books of history that are among the oldest books in existence.

Historical passages concerning the fate of nations, their relations with each other, and the causes for their decline and fall, occur frequently in the Qur'an; they must be studied by the historian with a historical and scientific approach. The sociologist must examine them according to sociological method. Cosmological matters and questions relating to the natural sciences and natural phenomena must be examined and understood according to the methodology of the natural sciences.

Since my area of study and specialization is history and sociology, I assume the right to set forth what has occurred to me in this connection as a plan or design. I will set forth two methods, both of them relating exclusively to the vantage point of sociology, history and the human sciences. In order to make my meaning clearer, I will compare religion to an individual.

Only two ways exist in which to acquire knowledge of a great personality, and both of these ways must be pursued simultaneously in order to yield the final result—the knowledge of the great man in question.

The first way consists of studying and investigating the intellectual, scientific and written works of the individual, his theories, his speeches, his lectures and his books. Knowledge of the ideas and beliefs of a person is an indispensable preliminary to understanding him. But our investigation of these will not suffice for a complete understanding of the person, because many things will exist in his life that are not reflected in his works, his writings and his pronouncements, or, if reflected there, they may be difficult to discern. The second way, which complements the first and makes possible a complete understanding of the person, is to study his biography and to seek an answer to such questions as: where was he born? to what family did he belong? what was his race and what was his country? how did his childhood pass? how was he educated? in what environment did he grow up? where did he study? who were his teachers? what events did he confront in the course of his life? what were his failures and his successes?

There are, then, two fundamental methods for gaining knowledge of a person, and both must be followed: first, the investigation of his thoughts and beliefs; and second, the examination of his biography from beginning to end.

A religion is like a person. The ideas of a religion are concentrated in its book, its "scripture," the very foundation of the school of thought to which it summons men. As for the biography of a religion, it is its history.

There are, then, two fundamental methods for learning Islam correctly, precisely and in accordance with contemporary methodology. First, the study of the Qur'an, taking it as the compendium of the ideas and the scientific and literary output of the person known as "Islam"; and second, the study of Islamic history, taking it as the sum total of the developments undergone by Islam from the beginning of the Prophet's mission down to the present.

These are the two methods, but unfortunately the study of the Qur'an and the study of Islamic history are very weak, as they now exist in our corpus of Islamic studies; in fact, they exist on the fringe of those studies. Fortunately, however, as a result of the awakening that has taken place in Muslim society in our age, Muslims are paying increased attention to the study of the Qur'anic text and to the analytical study of Islamic history.

In his book *The Night of Imperialism,* Farhat Abbas says that the social awakening of the countries of North Africa—Morocco, Algeria and Tunis—began on the day that Muhammad Abduh came to North Africa and began teaching the interpretation of the Qur'an, a subject that had not customarily been taught in the circles of religious learning.

We see that the author of the book—who was not himself religiously oriented—regards the beginning of awakening and religious development in the countries of North Africa as having occurred when the Muslims and their religious scholars laid aside the study of the various religious sciences and made it their chief concern to go back to the Qur'an and study its text.

The knowledge and understanding of the Qur'an as the source of the ideas of Islam, and the knowledge and understanding of Islamic history as the record of the various events that have occurred at different times—these are the two fundamental methods for attaining a precise and scientific knowledge of Islam.

If today the Muslims of Iran are transforming their mosques into centers of activity and are drawing up plans for the instruction of the masses, on the twin bases of the Qur'an and history, they will have laid the firmest foundation possible for a great Islamic intellectual expansion and development.

Another method exists for gaining knowledge and understanding of Islam—the method of typology. This method, which many sociologists believe effective, consists of classifying topics and themes according to type and then comparing them on that basis.

Based on this approach, which is used in Europe in research on certain topics pertaining to the human sciences, I have established a method that can be applied to every religion. It consists of the identification of five distinguishing aspects or characteristics of every religion, and then comparing them with the corresponding features in other religions:

1) the god or gods of every religion; i.e., the entity worshipped by the followers of the religion.

2) the prophet of each religion; i.e., the person who proclaims the message of the religion.

3) the book of each religion; i.e., the foundation of the law proclaimed by the religion, to which it invites men in faith and obedience.

4) the circumstances of the appearance of the prophet of each religion and the audience to which he addresses himself; for each prophet proclaims his message in a different fashion. One will address himself to people in general (*al-nas*), another to princes and the nobility, and still another to the learned, the philosophers and the elect. One prophet will thus seek to draw near to established power, while another sets himself up as an adversary and opponent to established power.

5) those choice individuals each religion nurtures and produces—the representative figures it has trained and then presented to society and history. In just the same way that the best method for assessing a factory is to inspect the goods it produces, and for assessing a plot of land is to examine the harvest it yields, so too religion may be regarded as a factory for the production of men, and the men nurtured by each religion constitute the goods it produces.

According to this method, in order to learn and know more of Islam, one must first know God or Allah. Various ways exist for gaining knowledge of God, such as gazing and meditating upon nature and the methods of philosophy, illumination and gnosis. . . . But the method I wish to propose is that of typology. We examine the type, concept, features and characteristics of the God discussed in Islam. For example, we ask whether He is wrathful or merciful. Is He exalted above all being? Is He commingled with man? Does His compassionate aspect predominate over His wrathful aspect, or is the reverse the case? In short, what "type" of God is He?

In order to correctly recognize the characteristics of God, we must refer to the Qur'an and the words of the Prophet, as well as the elite among those whom he trained. For the divine attributes have been clearly set forth in the Qur'an, and the Prophet and those whom he trained have referred to them in their pronouncements. Then we can compare Allah with the figure depicted in other religions as God—Ahuramazda, Yahwa, Zeus, Baal, and so forth.

The second stage in knowing and learning Islam consists in knowing and learning its book, the Qur'an. One must also understand what kind of a book the Qur'an is, what topics it discusses, and what areas it emphasizes. Does it speak more of the life of this world or more of the hereafter? Does it discuss questions of individual morality more, or social questions? Is it concerned more with material or with abstract objects? Is it more interested in nature or in man? In short, what matters does it treat and in what fashion?

For example, with respect to proving the existence of God, does it recommend to man that he should refine his soul in order to know God? Or does it instruct us to attain knowledge of God through the study of the particulars of creation, the external and internal worlds? Or should we follow both paths?

Havings answered these questions, we should proceed to a comparison of the Qur'an with other religious texts, such as the Gospels, the Torah, the Vedas, the Avesta, and so on.

The third stage in acquiring knowledge of Islam is learning the personality of Muhammad ibn Abdullah. To know and understand the Prophet of Islam is extremely important for the historian, for nobody has played in human history the same role as the Prophet. The role of the Prophet in the events he occasioned is an extremely powerful and positive one. When we speak of the personality of the Prophet, we mean both his human attributes and his relationship with God, with the particular spiritual strength he derived therefrom. In other words, we are concerned both with his human and his prophetic aspects.

For example, with the human dimension of the Prophet, we must study the way in which he spoke, worked, thought, smiled, sat and slept; we must study the nature of his relations with strangers, with enemies, with friends and family. We must also examine his failures and his triumphs and the manner in which he confronted great social problems. One of the basic and fundamental ways of learning the original essence, spirit and reality of Islam is, then, learning about the Prophet of Islam and comparing him with other prophets and founders of religions, like Moses, Jesus, Zoroaster and the Buddha.

The fourth stage consists of examining the circumstances under which the Prophet of Islam appeared. Did he, for example, appear without any preliminary? Was anyone waiting for him? Did he himself anticipate his mission? Did he know what his mission was to be? Or was it that a sudden and powerful blow descended upon his spirit, an extraordinary current of thought began to flow through his mind, totally changing his manner of speech and personality, in such fashion that he initially found it difficult to bear? How did he confront men when he first proclaimed his mission? To what class did he pay particular attention, and against what class did he struggle? All of these are matters that aid us in the understanding of the Prophet of Islam and the circumstances of his appearance.

If we compare the circumstances under which the Prophet of Islam appeared with those under which other prophets appeared—whether true or false—such as Jesus, Abraham, Moses, Zoroaster, Confucius, Buddha and so forth, we reach the following remarkable conclusion: all the prophets, with the exception of those of the Abrahamic line, turn immediately to the existing secular power and seek association with it, hoping to propagate their religion and message in society by means of that power. By contrast, all the prophets of the Abrahamic line, from Abraham down to the Prophet of Islam, proclaim their missions in the form of rebellion against the existing secular power. At the very outset of his mission, Abraham begins destroying idols with his ax; he strikes his ax against the supreme idol of his people in order to proclaim his opposition to all the idols of his age. The first sign of the mission of Moses is when he enters the court of the Pharaoh in his shepherd's garb, with his staff in hand, and declares war on pharaonism in the name of monotheism. Similarly, Jesus struggles against the power of the Jewish priesthood, since it is allied with Roman imperialism. And the Prophet of Islam, at the very beginning of his mission, starts the struggle against the aristocracy, the slaveowners and the merchants of Quraysh, the owners of orchards in Ta'if. The comparison of the two groups of prophets—the Abrahamic and the non-Abrahamic—helps us to understand the essence, spirit and orientation of the various religions in question.

The fifth stage in the learning and understanding of Islam consists in studying the outstanding examples, the finest goods that these factories for the production of men have delivered to humanity, society and history.

If, for example, we choose to study Aaron in the religion of Moses, St. Paul in the religion of Jesus, and Ali, Husayn or Abu Dharr in the religion of Islam, as outstanding specimens of each of the religions, this will facilitate for us the understanding of the religions.

An exact, clear knowledge of those persons will, from the scientific point of view, resemble the knowledge of a factory through the knowledge of the goods it produces, because religion is a factory engaged in the production of men.

Let us tonight take Husayn as the example of one trained and nurtured by the religion of Islam, in order to discover what kind of a man it is who believes in Allah, the Qur'an and the Prophet.

The life of Husayn is well known, as are the principles for which he fought. His sensitivity with respect to social matters and the destiny of the people, his devotion and self-sacrifice— these, too, are well known. It is well known, further, when the truth and what he believed in were threatened, how easily he renounced and sacrificed all that a man is attached to in the course of his worldly life. He was, in short, such a person that we can designate Husayn the son of Ali as an outstanding example for the purposes of our study.

In addition to learning and acquiring a knowledge of the life, ideas, and characteristics of Husayn, another method also presents itself to us. This is to compare Husayn with Abu Ali Sina and Husayn b. Mansur Hallaj, who were Muslim but trained and nurtured by philosophy and Iranian Sufism respectively.

The comparison of these three individuals will help us to gain a vivid comprehension of the differences between the schools of philosophy, Sufism and Islam, as well as their common features.

Ibn Sina was a great philosopher, scholar and genius, a source of pride to the whole history of science and philosophy in Islamic civilization. But this great and profound man, who was so outstanding as a philosopher and scholar, was content, from the social point of view, to place himself in the service of rank and of power, and he never showed any concern with the destiny of man and the fate of his society. He saw no connection between his own fate and that of others. His sole concerns were the investigation of scientific matters and scholarly research. The outer form of his life was a matter of indifference for him; whoever granted him money and position was acceptable to him.

As for Hallaj, he was a man aflame. A man that is on fire has no responsibility; it is his function simply to burn and to cry out. Why was Hallaj burning? From the passionate love of God. He had taken his head between his hands and run through the streets of Baghdad proclaiming, "Split open this head, for it has rebelled against me! Deliver me from this fire that is burning within me! I am nothing, I am God!" By this he meant, "I no longer exist, God alone exists!"

Hallaj was constantly immersed in the burning invocation of God, and this was a source of true exaltation for him. But imagine if Iranian society were to consist of 25 million Hallaj's. It would be nothing but a vast lunatic asylum, with everyone running into the streets proclaiming, "Come, kill me! I can endure it no longer! I have nothing! There is naught in my cloak but God!"

Such instances of burning passion and immersion represent a kind of spiritual or mystical lunacy, and if all the members of society were like Hallaj—or, for that matter, like Ibn Sina—the result would be wretchedness and destruction.

But now imagine a society in which only one Husayn son of Ali exists, together with several Abu Dharrs. That society would have life and liberty, thought and learning, power and stability; it would be capable both of defeating its enemies and of truly loving God.

A translation of Insan va Islam, *a lecture given at the Petroleum College of Abadan. The introductory paragraph has been omitted.*

Man and Islam

THE QUESTION OF MAN is the most important of all questions. The civilization of today is based upon humanism, the nobility of man and the worship of man. It is believed that the religions of the past crushed the personality of man and compelled him to sacrifice himself to the gods. They forced him to regard his own will as totally powerless when confronted by the will of God. They compelled him always to be seeking something from God by way of prayer, supplication and entreaty. The philosophy of humanism is, then, a philosophy that, since the Renaissance, has opposed religious philosophies —philosophies founded on belief in the unseen and supranatural realm—and its aim has allegedly been to restore nobility to man. The roots of humanism lie in Athens, but as a universal philosophy, it has become the basis of the modern civilization of the West. In reality, it arose as a reaction to scholastic philosophy and medieval Christianity.

My purpose tonight is to examine—within the limits of my capability and the present occasion—the question of man from the viewpoint of our religion, Islam, and to seek an answer to the question: what kind of a phenomenon does Islam see in man? Does it see in man a powerless creature whose ultimate aim and ideal is to stand helpless before God? Does Islam deny man all notion of nobility? Or, on the contrary, does belief in Islam itself impart a form of nobility to man, and make an acknowledgement of his virtues? This is the topic I wish to discuss.

In order to understand the place of "humanism" in different religions, and the concept of man that each of them holds, it is best to study the philosophy of the creation of man that each has set forth. However, I do not have the opportunity now to examine all the religions of East and West from this point of view. I will speak only of the philosophy of creation that exists in Islam and those pre-Islamic religions of which Islam is the continuation—the religions of Moses, Jesus and Abraham.

How is the creation of man explained in Islam or the Abrahamic scriptures, of which Islam is the culmination and perfection? Can we deduce the status and nature of man from the manner in which the creation of man is described in the Qur'an, the Word of God, or in the words of the Prophet of Islam? From examining the story of Adam—the symbol of man—in the Qur'an, we can understand what kind of a creature man is in the view of God and therefore in the view of our religion. By way of introduction, let me point out that the language of religion, and particularly the language of the semitic religions, in whose prophets we believe, is a symbolical language. By this we mean a language that expresses meaning through images and symbols—the most excellent and exalted of all the languages that men have ever evolved. Its value is more profound and eternal than that of expository language, i.e., the clear and explicit language that expresses meaning directly. A simple and straightforward language, one deprived of all symbol and image, may be easier for purposes of instruction, but it has no permanence. For, as the celebrated Egyptian philosopher Abd ar-Rahman Badawi has pointed out, a religion or philosophy that expounds all of its ideas and teachings in simple, one-dimensional and straightforward language will not be able to survive. Those addressed by religion or philosophy represent different human types and classes—both the common folk and the educated. The audience of a religion is, moreover, not a single generation or age, but different and successive generations which follow upon each other throughout history. They inevitably differ with each other with respect to way of thought, level of thought, and angle of vision. The language that a religion chooses in order to convey its concepts must, then, be a versatile and multi-faceted language, each aspect and facet of which addresses itself to a particular generation and class of men. If the language be monofaceted, it will be comprehensible only to a single class, and totally without value for all other classes; accessible to one generation, but beyond the reach of the next. It will be impossible to extract any new meaning from it. It is for this reason that all literary works written in symbolic language are immortal. For example, the poems of Hafiz are immortal, and whenever we read them we deduce a new meaning from them, in proportion to the depth of our thought and taste and outlook. But the history of Bayhaqi is something different, as is, too, the *Gulistan* of Sa'di. When we read the *Gulistan*, its meaning is quite apparent to us, and we enjoy its verbal beauty and structure. But many of the ideas it contains are outmoded, precisely because it is clear what Sa'di had to say, and what he had to say is false! But the style of Hafiz is multi-faceted and symbolical; depending on his taste and manner of thought, everyone can interpret its symbols in a certain sense, thus deducing new meanings from the text.

It is for this reason that religions must employ a symbolic language; they are addressed to different human types and different generations of men. There are numerous concepts in religion that were not clearly understood at the time of their appearance. If religion had *not*, on the one hand, expressed its ideas in common, familiar language, it would have been incomprehensible to the people of that age; but if it *had* expressed its ideas in common language, religion would have had no meaning in later times. It was therefore necessary that religion should speak in images and symbols that would become comprehensible with the development of human thought and science. Symbolism represents the highest of styles in European literature—symbolism, which is the art of speaking in symbols and images and concealing profound ideas in images that apparently mean something else but have an inner significance that man can discover in accordance with his own degree of profundity.

It was necessary, then, that the story of the creation of Adam, of man, be told in symbolic fashion, so that today, after fourteen centuries of progress in the human and natural sciences, it should still be readable and comprehensible.

How was man created, in the view of Islam?

First God addresses the angels, saying, "I wish to create a viceregent for Myself upon earth." See how great is the value of man according to Islam! Even the post-Renaissance humanism of Europe has never been able to conceive of such exalted sanctity for man. God, Who in the view of Islam and all believers, is the greatest and most exalted of all entities, the creator of Adam and the master of the cosmos, addresses the angels and presents man to them as His viceregent. The whole mission of man according to Islam becomes evident from this divine address. The same mission that God has in the cosmos, man must perform on earth as God's viceregent. The first excellence that man possesses is, then, being God's representative on earth.

The angels cry out saying, "You wish to create one who will engage in bloodshed, crime, hatred and vengeance." (Since before Adam, there had been other men who, like the man of today, busied themselves in bloodshed, crime, corruption and sin, and the angels wished to remind God that if He were to create man again and grant him a second opportunity on earth, man would again engage in bloodshed and sin.) But God replies, "I know something that you do not know," and then sets about the task of creating man.

It is at this point that the symbolic aspect of the narrative begins. See what profound truths concerning man are hidden beneath these symbols! God desires to create a viceregent for Himself out of earth, the face of the globe. One might expect that the most sacred and valuable of materials would have been selected, but God chose, on the contrary, the lowest of substances. The Qur'an mentions on three occasions the substance from which man was fashioned. First it uses the expression "like potter's clay" (55:14); that is, dry, sedimentary clay. Then the Qur'an says, "I created man from putrid clay" (15:26), foul and evil-smelling earth; and finally it uses the term *tin*, also meaning clay (6:2, 23:12). So God set to work, and willed to create a viceregent for Himself; this precious viceregent He created out of dry clay, and then He inhaled some of his own spirit into the clay, and man was created.

In human language, the lowest symbol of wretchedness and baseness is mud. No creature exists in nature lowlier than mud.

Again in human language, the most exalted and sacred of beings is God, and the most exalted, sacred and noble part of every being is its spirit. Man, the representative of God, was created from mud, from sedimentary clay, from the lowliest substance in the world, and then God inhaled into him not His blood or His body—so to speak—but His spirit, the most exalted entity for which human languages possess a name. God is the most exalted of beings, and His spirit is the most exalted entity conceivable, the most exalted concept that could ever arise in the human mind.

Thus man is a compound of mud and divine spirit, a bi-dimensional being, a creature with a dual nature, as opposed to all other beings which are one-dimensional. One dimension inclines to mud and lowliness, to stagnation and immobility. When a river overflows, it leaves behind a certain muddy sediment that lacks all motion and life, and the nature of man, in one of its dimensions, aspires to precisely this state of sedimentary tranquility. But the other dimension, that of the divine spirit, as it is called in the Qur'an, aspires to ascend and to mount up to the highest summit conceivable—to God and the spirit of God.

Man is composed, then, of two contradictory elements, mud and the spirit of God; and his splendor and importance derive precisely from the fact that he is a two-dimensional creature. The distance between his two dimensions is the distance between clay and the spirit of God. Every man is endowed with these two dimensions, and it is his will that enables him to decide either to descend toward the pole of sedimentary mud that exists in his being, or to ascend toward the pole of exaltation, of God and the spirit of God. This constant striving and struggle takes place in man's inner being, until finally he chooses one of the poles as the determinant for his destiny.

After thus creating man, God taught him the names. (As will be apparent to you, I am paraphrasing the verses of the Qur'an as I proceed.) What does this teaching of the names mean? It is not yet certain. Everyone has expressed a certain opinion, and every commentator has suggested his own interpretation. Everyone has interpreted it according to his own outlook and way of thought. But whatever be the correct explanation, there can be no doubt that the verse centers on the notion of teaching and instruction. When the creation of man was completed, God taught His viceregent the names so that man became a possessor of the names. Then the angels cried out in protest, "We were created of smokeless fire and man was created of clay; why do you prefer him to us?" And God replies, "I know something you do not know; fall down at the feet of this two-dimensional creature of mine." All the angels of God, great and small, are commanded to fall down in prostration before this creature.

This is true humanism. See how great is the dignity and stature of man; so great, indeed, that all the angels, despite their inherent superiority to man and the fact that they are created of light while he is created of mud and clay, are commanded to fall down before him. God tests them because of their protest, and asks the angels concerning the names; they do not know the names, but Adam does know them. The angels are defeated in this test, and the excellence of Adam—which lies in his knowledge of the names—becomes apparent. This prostration of the angels before Adam serves to clarify the Islamic concept of man. Man knows certain things that the angels do not know, and this knowledge endows man with superiority to the angels despite the superiority of the angels to man with respect to race and origin. In other words, the nobility and dignity of man derive from knowledge and not from lineage.

Another point to be considered is the creation of woman from the rib of man, at least according to the translations usually made from the Arabic.[1] But the translation "rib" is incorrect, and the word so translated has the real meaning, in both Arabic and Hebrew, of "nature, disposition or constitution." Eve—that is, woman—was created, then, out of the same nature or disposition as man. Since the word has been mistranslated as "rib," the legend arose that woman was created from the left rib of Adam, and therefore all women are lacking one rib!

---

[1] The creation of Eve is not directly mentioned in the Qur'an, so the author is presumably referring to accounts such as that given in Kisa'i's *Qisas al-Anbiya*, Cairo, 1312, pp. 18 ff. (TR.)

A great man like Nietzsche said that man and woman were created as totally separate creatures, and only came to resemble each other because of their constant association through history. The ancestries of man and woman he held to be totally different. Almost all scholars and philosophers have conceded that man and woman are of the same stock, yet they have always tried to belittle the nature of woman and present the nature of man as superior. But the Qur'an says, "We have created Eve from the same nature or disposition as Adam; man and woman proceed from the same substance."

Another remarkable matter concerning the creation of man is that God summons all of His creation, all the phenomena of nature such as inanimate objects, plants, animals, and tells them, "I have a trust that I wish to offer to all of you—earth, heavens, mountains, oceans and beasts." They all refuse to accept it, and instead, man accepts it. It is thus clear that man has another virtue and excellence, deriving from his courageous acceptance of the Trust that God offered to all beings and they rejected. Man is not only the viceregent of God in this world and on this earth, but also—as the Qur'an makes clear—the keeper of His Trust. Now what is the meaning of the Trust? Everyone says something different. Maulana Jalal ad-Din Rumi says that the Trust means man's will, his free will, and this is also my opinion.

It is by means of his will that man attains superiority over all other creatures in the world. He is the only being able to act counter to his own instinctual nature, something no animal or plant can do. For example, you will never encounter an animal voluntarily engaging in a two-day fast, or a plant committing suicide out of grief. Plants and animals can neither render great services nor commit treachery. It is not possible for them to act in a way different from that in which they have been created. It is only man who can rebel against the way in which he was created, who can defy even his spiritual or bodily needs, and act against the dictates of goodness and virtue. He can act either in accordance with his intelligence or in opposition to it. He is free to be good or to be evil, to resemble mud or to resemble God. Will is, then, the greatest property of man, and the affinity between God and man is apparent from this fact.

For it is God Who inhales into man some of His own spirit and makes of him the bearer of His Trust, and man is not merely the viceregent of God upon earth but also His relative—if the expression be permitted. The spirits of God and man both possess an excellence deriving from the possession of will. God, the only entity and being possessing an absolute will and capable of doing whatever it wishes, even in contradiction to the laws of the universe, inhales some of His spirit in man. Man can act like God, but only to a certain degree; he can act against the laws of his physiological constitution only to the extent permitted by his similarity to God. This is the aspect held in common by men and God, the cause of their affinity—free will, the freedom for man to be good or evil, to obey or rebel.

The following conclusions can be drawn with regard to the philosophy of the creation of man in Islam:

All men are not simply equal; they are brothers. The difference between equality and brotherhood is quite clear. Equality is a legal concept, while brotherhood proclaims the uniform nature and disposition of all men; all men originate from a single source, whatever their color.

Secondly, man and woman are equal. Contrary to all the philosophies of the ancient world, man and woman were created out of the same substance and material at the same time and by the same Creator. They share the same lineage, and are brothers and sisters to each other, descended from the same mother and father.

Thirdly, the superiority of man to the angels and the whole of creation derives from knowledge, since man learned the names and the angels fell in prostration before him; despite the superiority of their descent to that of man, they were compelled to humble themselves before him.

More important than all this, man's being stretches out over the distance between mud and God, and since he possesses will, he can choose either of the two opposing poles these represent. Again since he possesses will, a certain responsibility comes into being. From the point of view of Islam, man is the only being responsible not only for his own destiny but also for the fulfillment of a divinely entrusted mission in this world; he is the bearer of God's Trust in the world and in nature. It is he who

has learned the names—and, in my opinion, the proper meaning of "names" is the truths of science, since the name of a thing
is its symbol, its defined, conceptual form. The teaching of the
names by God means, therefore, the bestowal of the ability to
perceive and comprehend the scientific truths inherent in the
world. Through this primordial instruction by God, man
gained access to all the truths existing in the world, and this
constitutes a second great responsibility for man. Man must
fashion his destiny with his own hands. Human society is
responsible for its own fate, and the human individual is
responsible for his own fate: "Yours is what you acquire and
theirs is what they acquire" (Qur'an, 2:134). The fate of past
civilizations is no more and no less than what they brought
down on themselves, and your fate will consist exactly of what
you are now fashioning with your own hands. Man thus has a
great responsibility toward God, since he possesses free will.

Here we must add this observation, that history has witnessed
a great tragedy; namely, man has not been recognized as a
two-dimensional being. In contrast with other religions that
posit God and the Devil to exist within nature in mutual
combat, Islam teaches that only one force exists in nature—the
force of God. But within man, Satan wages war against God,
and man is their battlefield. The dualism of Islam, unlike
religions of the past, posits the existence of two "deities," two
hypostases, in the inner being and disposition of man, not in
nature. Nature knows only of a single hypostasis; it belongs to
the realm, and is subject to the will, of a single power, the power
of God. In Islam, Satan is not a contestant with God; he is a
contestant against man, or rather against the divine half of
man. And since man is a two-dimensional creature composed of
God and of clay, he has need of both elements. The religion and
ideology that he needs to believe in and to found his life upon
must fulfill both kinds of need and pay both of them due
attention. The tragedy is that history tells a different tale. History tells us that all societies and civilizations were oriented
exclusively either to the hereafter and renunciation of this
world, or to this world of dust. The civilization of China began
by being oriented to this world, by giving primacy to pleasure

and beauty and striving to enjoy the gifts of nature to the full, as the life of the Chinese aristocracy testifies. Then came Lao Tse, bringing a religion exclusively oriented to the hereafter, and emphasizing the spiritual and other-wordly dimension of man. Indeed, he led the Chinese so far in that direction, that a people who had lived purely for the sake of pleasure became monks, gnostics and mystics. He was succeeded by Confucius, who reoriented society toward this world and summoned the Chinese to the pleasures of worldly life, causing them to revert to their former preoccupations.

India, the land of rajas and legends, was oriented to the other world by the teachings of the Vedas and the Buddha, devoting itself to abstemiousness, monasticism and mysticism. It is for this reason that India is now famous for men sleeping on beds of nails, or subsisting for forty days on a single date or almond, for remaining behind the progress of civilization.

In Europe, ancient Rome devoted itself to murder and bloodshed, to establishing political mastery of the world, to accumulating all the wealth of Europe and Asia; it immersed itself in enjoyment and pleasure, in gladiator fights and the like. Then came Jesus, who directed society to concentrate on the hereafter, so that Rome changed its orientation from pleasure and worldliness to asceticism and contemplation of the hereafter, the ultimate result of this being the Middle Ages. The medieval world was one of war and bloodshed and military ascendance on the one hand; and one of monasteries, nunneries and retreats, on the other. Europe was delivered from this orientation only by the Renaissance, which caused the pendulum to swing in the other direction. Today we see that European civilization is so worldly in its orientation, and so exclusively defines the purpose of man's life as pleasure and enjoyment, that, as Professor Chandel has put it, the life of contemporary man consists only of making the tools of life. This is the idiocy of the contemporary philosophy of man, the result of a purpose-free technology. The whole meaning of civilization has been robbed of any ideal, and the world has gone so far in the direction of worldliness that it almost seems as if another Jesus were needed.

As is apparent from the philosophy of man in Islam, he is a two-dimensional being and needs, therefore, a religion which will also be two-dimensional and exert its force in the two different and opposing directions that exist in man's spirit and human society. Only then will man be able to maintain his equilibrium. The religion needed is Islam.

Why Islam?

In order to understand any religion, one must study its God, its Book, its Prophet, and the best individuals whom it has nurtured and raised.

First, the God of Islam is a two-dimensional God. He has the aspect of Yahwa, the god of the Jews, who interests himself in human society, in the affairs of this world, who is stern, severe in punishment, and tyrannical, and also the aspect of the god of Jesus, who is compassionate, merciful and forgiving. All of these divine attributes can be found in the Qur'an.

As for the book of Islam, the Qur'an, it is a book that like the Torah contains social, political and military provisions, even instructions for the conduct of warfare, the taking and setting free of prisoners; that is interested in life, in building, in prosperity, in struggling against enemies and negative elements; but it is also a book that concerns itself with the refinement of the soul, the piety of the spirit, and the ethical improvement of the individual.

The Prophet of Islam also possesses two contrasting aspects, aspects which would be contradictory in other men, but in him have been joined in a single spirit. For he was a man constantly engaged in political struggle against his enemies and the dis-ruptive forces in society, concerned with building a new society and a new civilization in this world; and also a guide leading men to a particular goal; that is, also a man of prayer, piety and devotion.

And then three men trained by him—Ali, Abu Dharr and Salman—were supreme examples of two-dimensional men. They were both men of politics and battle, struggling for a better life and constantly present in circles of discussion and learning, and also men of piety and purity, not less than the great monks and mystics of the East. Abu Dharr was a man of politics and piety; the reflections of Abu Dharr concerning the nature of God can serve as a key to the understanding of the Qur'an. Look at all the Companions of the Prophet; they were all men of the sword, concerned with improving their society, men of justice, and at the same time, great men of thought and feeling.

The conclusion I wish to draw is this: in Islam man is not humbled before God, for he is the partner of God, His friend, the bearer of His trust upon earth. He enjoys affinity with God, has been instructed by Him, and seen all of God's angels fall prostrate before him. Two-dimensional man, bearing the burden of such responsibility, needs a religion that transcends exclusive orientation to this world or the next, and permits him to maintain a state of equilibrium. It is only such a religion that enables man to fulfill his great responsibility.

Translated from Islamshinasi, *Vol. I, pp. 46-56.*

The World-View of Tauhid

MY WORLD-VIEW CONSISTS OF *tauhid. Tauhid* in the sense of oneness of God is of course accepted by all monotheists. But *tauhid* as a world-view in the sense I intend in my theory means regarding the whole universe as a unity, instead of dividing it into this world and the hereafter, the natural and the supernatural, substance and meaning, spirit and body. It means regarding the whole of existence as a single form, a single living and conscious organism, possessing will, intelligence, feeling and purpose. There are many people who believe in *tauhid*, but only as a religious-philosophical theory, meaning nothing but "God is one, not more than one." But I take *tauhid* in the sense of a world-view, and I am convinced that Islam also intends it in this sense. I regard *shirk* in a similar fashion; it is a world-view that regards the universe as a discordant assemblage full of disunity, contradiction, and heterogeneity, possessing a variety of independent and clashing poles, conflicting tendencies, variegated and unconnected desires, reckonings, customs, purposes and wills. *Tauhid* sees the world as an empire; *shirk* as a feudal system.

The difference between my world-view and that of materialism or naturalism lies in this, that I regard the world as a living being, endowed with will and self-awareness, percipient, and having an ideal and a purpose. Existence is therefore a living being, possessing a single and harmonious order that is endowed with life, will, sensation and purpose, just like a vast and absolute man (man likewise resembles the world, but a small, relative and defective world). To put it differently, if we take a man endowed with awareness, creativity and purpose, exemplary to the utmost degree in all of his aspects, and then enlarge him to the utmost degree, we will have before us the world.

The relationship of man with God, of nature with metanature, of nature with God (all of these are terms I use reluctantly), is the same as that of light with the lamp that emits it. It is also the same as the relationship between an individual's awareness of his limb and the limb itself: his perception is not separate from his limb, nor is it alien to it; but neither is it part of the limb, and still less, the limb itself. At the same time, the limb itself, without his consciousness of it, is a meaningless corpse.[1] So it is that I do not believe in pantheism, polytheism, trinitarianism, or dualism, but only in *tauhid*—monotheism. *Tauhid* represents a particular view of the world that demonstrates a universal unity in existence, a unity between three separate hypostases—God, nature, and man—because the origin of all three is the same.[2] All have the same direction, the same will, the same spirit, the same motion, and the same life.

In this world-view of *tauhid*, being is divided into two relative aspects: the unseen and the manifest. These two terms correspond in current usage to the sensible and the suprasensible, or, more exactly, to that which lies beyond the scope of examination, observation and experiment (and hence knowledge) and is hidden from our sense-perception, and that which is manifest and observable. This does not represent a form of

---

[1] How profound, beautiful and clear are the words of Hazrat Ali: "God is outside of things, but not in the sense of being alien to them; and He is inside things, but not in the sense of being identical with them."

[2] It hardly needs stating that I do not intend here a substantial unity in essence and quiddity. Do not permit these philosophical and theological terms to tire your brain; simply expel them from your mind. For I am convinced that this is the only thing to do with this kind of apparently insoluble philosophical-literary problem. My meaning in saying that God, nature and man have the same origin is that they are not remote from each other, not alien to each other, not opposed to each other, and that no boundary exists among them. They do not have each a separate and independent direction. Other religions believe that God exists in a special, metaphysical world of the gods, a higher world contrasting with the lower world of nature and matter. They also teach that the God of man is separate and distinct from the God of nature. Thus God, the world and man are all separate from each other! We do not accept this separation.

dualism or bisection of being; it is a relative classification—
relative to man and his means of cognition. The division into
unseen and manifest is, in reality, an epistemological one, not
an ontological one. It is also a logical division, not only
accepted but also applied by science.

The materialists believe in the primacy of matter as the
original and primordial substance of the physical world, and
regard energy as the product and the changing form of matter.
The energists claim that on the contrary, energy is the primary
and eternal substance of the physical world, and that matter is
the changed and compressed form of energy. In opposition to
both groups, Einstein proclaimed that an experiment in a
darkened room proves that neither matter nor energy is the
primary and true source of the world of being. The two inter-
change with each other in such a way as to prove that they are
the alternating manifestations of an invisible and unknowable
essence that sometimes shows itself in the form of matter and
sometimes in the form of energy. The only task of physics is to
examine these twin manifestations of the one suprasensible
being.

In the world-view of *tauhid*, nature, the manifest world, is
composed of a series of signs (*ayat*) and norms (*sunan*).

The use of the word "sign" (*aya*) to designate a natural
phenomenon bears profound meaning. The oceans and trees,
night and day, earth and sun, earthquake and death, illness,
vicissitude, law, and even man himself—all these are "signs."
At the same time, "sign" and "God" do not represent two
separate and discordant hypostases, essences, realms, or poles.
"Sign" has the sense of indication or manifestation, and this in
turn is synonymous with a term current today, not only in
physics but all the sciences concerned with the tangible world—
"phenomenon," translated in Persian as *padida* or *padidar,* and
in Arabic as *zahira.* Phenomenology, in its most general sense,
is based on the recognition that absolute truth, the ground and
essence of the world, of nature and of matter, lies beyond our
grasp. What is knowable and accessible to our experience,
knowledge and sense-perception, is "appearance," not "being"; it consists of the outer and sensible manifestations and

traces of a primary, unseen and suprasensory reality. Physics, chemistry and psychology can examine, analyze and render knowable these outer manifestations and sensible indications of the true essence of the world and the soul. In short, science deals with the signs, indications and manifestations of being, because sensible nature is the amalgam of these signs and manifestations.

Among all the books of religion, science and philosophy, it is only the Qur'an that designates all the objects, accidents and processes of nature as "signs." Of course, in Islamic mysticism as well as oriental pantheism, the material world has been depicted as a series of waves or bubbles on the face of the vast, colorless and formless ocean that is God or the true essence of being. Idealism and various religious and ethical philosophies have also regarded material nature as a collection of lowly and worthless objects opposed to both God and man. But the Qur'an assigns positive scientific worth to the "signs"; it does not consider them illusions, or veils over the face of the truth. On the contrary, they are indications pointing to the truth, and it is only by means of contemplating them in a serious and scientific fashion that one can attain the truth, not by ignoring them and thrusting them aside.

This manner of regarding the "signs" or phenomena of the world is closer to the approach of modern science than to that of ancient mysticism. It is not a question of the *wahdat al-wujud* of the Sufis, but a *tauhid-i wujud*, scientific and analytical. According to *tauhid*, multiplicity, plurality and contradiction are unacceptable, whether in history, society or even in man.

Tauhid, then, is to be interpreted in the sense of the unity of nature with metanature, of man with nature, of man with man, of God with the world and with man. It depicts all of these as constituting a total, harmonious, living and self-aware system.[3]

---

[3] The Light Verse (Qur'an, 24:35) illustrates this concept of being, since it demonstrates the special relationship between God and the world according to the world-view of *tauhid*. The whole of existence is like a burning lamp; this is neither "unity of being" (*wahdat al-wujud*) nor multiplicity of being, but *tauhid* of being.

I have said that the very structure of *tauhid* cannot accept contradiction or disharmony in the world. According to the world-view of *tauhid*, therefore, there is no contradiction in all of existence: no contradiction between man and nature, spirit and body, this world and the hereafter, matter and meaning. Nor can *tauhid* accept legal, class, social, political, racial, national, territorial, genetic or even economic contradictions, for it implies a mode of looking upon all being as a unity.

Contradiction between nature and metanature, matter and meaning, this world and the hereafter, the sensible and the suprasensible, spirit and body, intellect and illumination, science and religion, metaphysics and nature, working for men and working for God, politics and religion, logic and love, bread and worship, piety and commitment, life and eternity, landlord and peasant, ruler and ruled, black and white, noble and vile, clergy and laity, eastern and western, blessed and wretched, light and darkness, inherent virtue and inherent evil, Greek and barbarian, Arab and non-Arab, Persian and non-Persian, capitalist and proletarian, elite and mass, learned and illiterate—all these forms of contradiction are reconcilable only with the world-view of *shirk*—dualism, trinitarianism or polytheism—but not with *tauhid*—monotheism. It is for this reason that the world-view of *shirk* has always formed the basis for *shirk* in society, with its discrimination among classes and races. Belief in a plurality of creators justifies and sanctifies a plurality of creatures, presenting it as something eternal and everlasting.[4] Similarly, a belief in contradiction among the gods presents as natural and divine the contradictions existing among men. *Tauhid*, by contrast, which negates all forms of *shirk*, regards all the particles, processes and phenomena of existence as being engaged in harmonious movement toward a

---

[4] The term "Creator" in polytheistic religions implies something different from the term "Lord" or "God." Sometimes the gods themselves are created by a great Creator, while being at the same time entrusted with power and authority over a certain species or a certain sector of the world and human life. They have thus been worshipped by a certain class or race, and through their very multiplicity, have justified *shirk* among men.

single goal. Whatever is not oriented to that goal is by definition nonexistent.

One further consequence of the world-view of *tauhid* is the negation of the dependence of man on any social force, and the linking of him, in exclusivity and in all his dimensions, to the consciousness and will that rule over being. The source of support, orientation, belief, and succor of every individual is a single central point, a pivot around which revolve all the motions of the cosmos. All beings move in a circle described by luminous radii equidistant from the center, which is the powerful source of all being, the only will, the only consciousness, the only power that exists and rules over the universe. The position of man in this world is an objective embodiment of this truth, as is, more obviously, his circumambulation of the Ka'ba.

In the world-view of *tauhid,* man fears only one power, and is answerable before only one judge. He turns to only one *qibla,* and directs his hopes and desires to only one source. And the corollary is that all else is false and pointless—all the diverse and variegated tendencies, strivings, fears, desires and hopes of man are vain and fruitless.

Tauhid bestows upon man independence and dignity. Submission to Him alone—the supreme norm of all being—impels man to revolt against all lying powers, all the humiliating fetters of fear and of greed.

Translated from Islamshinasi, *Vol. I, pp. 56-68.*

Anthropology: The Creation of Man and the Contradiction of God and Iblis, or Spirit and Clay

T HE STORY OF ADAM and his creation in the Qur'an is the most profound and advanced expression of humanism that exists. In this story, Adam represents the whole human species, the essence of the human race, man in his philosophical sense, not in the biological sense. When the Qur'an speaks of man in the biological sense, it uses the language of the natural sciences, mentioning sperm, drops of clotted blood, fetus, etc. But when it comes to the creation of Adam, its language is metaphorical and philosophical, full of meaning and symbol. The creation of man, that is, the essence, spiritual destiny and attributes of the human race, as it appears in the story of Adam, may be reduced to the following formula:

The spirit of God + putrid clay = man

"Putrid clay" and the "spirit of God" are two symbols, or indications. It is not that man has actually been fashioned of putrid clay (*hama' masnun*) or of the spirit of God; rather, the first of the two terms refers to lowness, stagnation and absolute passivity, and the second indicates an endless movement toward perfection and infinite exaltation. "Spirit of God" is the best conceivable phrase for expressing this meaning.

The meaning of the Qur'anic statement that man is compounded from the spirit of God and putrid clay is similar to the assertion of Pascal in his book *Two Infinites,* that man is a being intermediate between two infinites: an infinity of lowliness and weakness, and an infinity of greatness and glory. There is, however, a great difference between the words of Pascal and the words of the Qur'an, even though they express the same truth; it is the same difference between Pascal and God!

The human situation, to use the terminology of existentialism, or the primordial disposition of man (*fitra*)—both terms signifying the dual and contradictory nature of man—can be deduced from the Qur'an as follows: man is a free and responsible will occupying a station intermediate between two opposing poles—God and Satan. The combination of these two opposites, the thesis and the antithesis, which exist both in man's nature and in his fate, create motion in him, a dialectic, ineluctable and evolutionary movement, and a constant struggle between the two opposing poles in man's essence and in his life.

The opposing, contradictory compound—God and Satan, or spirit and clay—that comprises man makes him a dialectic reality.[1]

God or the spirit of God, which represents absolute and infinite purity, beauty, splendor, power, creativity, awareness, vision, knowledge, love, mercy, will, freedom, independence, sovereignty and eternity, is present in man as a potentiality, an attraction that draws him toward the summit, to the glory of the heavens; as an ascension toward the sphere of God's sovereignty and being nurtured with the attributes and characteristics of

---

[1] I am, of course, aware that the joining of opposites is impossible, as is also the resolution of contradictions. But these rules pertain to Aristotelian logic, formal and abstract logic. Dialectics, however, has nothing to do with abstract forms, only with objective realities; it discusses not the motion of the mind and intellectual forms, but the objective motion of natural phenomena. In the world of the mind, it is impossible for an object to be hot and cold at the same time, or to be both large and small. In nature, however, this is not only possible, but actually obtains. The intellect cannot conceive of a being simultaneously dead and alive, because death and life cancel each other out, but in nature death and life exist with each other and within each other; they are the two sides of a single coin. A tree, an animal, a man, a social system, love, maternal tenderness— while all these are living and developing, they are also preparing their own old age and death. Hazrat Ali said: "The breaths a man takes are also the steps by which he advances toward death." The breath of life itself is a progress toward death.

God, as far as knowledge will reach. Aware of all the secrets of nature, man becomes a power enjoying kingship over the world; in front of him there bow down in submission all material and spiritual forces, earth and heaven, the sun and the moon, and even God's angels, including the highest among them. Man is thus a creature and a creator, a servant and a master; he is a conscious, seeing, creative, decisive, knowing, wise, purposeful, pure and exalted will, the bearer of God's trust and His viceregent on earth, an eternal creature of paradise.

How and why is this so? Half of man is the spirit of God; this is the thesis, the given, the fundament, that enables him to fly in ascension toward the absolute, toward God and divine character, that impels him to motion. There is, however, a powerful factor opposed to the first, which summons and drags him down to stagnation, solidity, immobility, death, lowliness and ugliness. Then man, who has a divine spirit which flows powerfully and tumultuously as a flood, which broadens and removes all obstacles in its path, causing verdure, gardens and fields to grow in its wake, before finally reaching the limpid waters of the ocean of eternity—then man will become the stagnant pools left behind by a flood. He will be unable to move; he will become stiff and hard and finally shatter, like the potter's sherds that cover the ground, blocking springs and stifling seeds. Nothing will grow from him; he will remain motionless and become a swamp instead of a field, a lagoon instead of an ocean; he will be stagnation instead of movement; death, instead of life; putrid clay, instead of the spirit of God— mud and sediment. The factor that brings all this about is the antithesis, that which negates and contradicts the thesis, what impels man in a direction opposed to the thesis.

From the combination of these two opposites, struggle and motion arise, as a result of which a perfecting synthesis comes into being.

The distance between the spirit of God and putrid clay is the distance between two infinities; and man is a "hesitation," a pendulum between them, a free will faced with a weighty and difficult choice—the choice of the spirit, the spirit of God, while contained within putrid clay and buried beneath mud and sediment.

In one direction lies the highest of the high—perfection, beauty, truth, power, awareness, absolute and infinite will— higher and greater than anything that might be imagined, beyond all that is lowly, banal, contemptible, commonplace, and petty—this is the hereafter. In the other direction lies the lowest of the low—defect, ugliness, falsity, weakness, ignorance, absolute bondage, an infinite decline—viler, uglier and more egoistic than anything that might be imagined—this is this world.

And in fact we see that men known to us have risen so far in brilliance of spirit, splendor, beauty, awareness, virtue, purity, courage, faith and generosity, and integrity of character, that they leave us amazed. No being material or immaterial, angel or jinn, has the capacity for similar growth. At the same time, we see other men who in their vileness, impurity, weakness, ugliness, cowardice and criminality have descended lower than any beast, microbe or demon. Man may attain the infinite in vileness, ugliness and evil just as he does in perfection, nobility and beauty. One extremity of man touches God; the other, the devil. Man is situated between two absolute possibilities, each situated at two extremities. He is a highway leading from "minus to the power of infinity" to "plus to the power of infinity." Facing him, traced out across the plain of being, is a highway leading from an infinitely vile minus to an infinitely exalted plus. He is a free and responsible will; he is both a will obliged to choose and the object of his own will and choice. To use the terminology of Brahmanism, he is the way, the wayfarer and the wayfaring. He is engaged in a constant migration from his self of clay to his divine self.

Man, this compound of opposites, is a dialectical being, a binary miracle of God.[2] In his essence and life-destiny, he is an

---

[2] The duality of God and Satan in Islam is not the same as the duality of God and Satan (the "bright Zurvan and the dark Zurvan") in dualistic religions such as Zoroastrianism and Manicheism. Further, it is not in any way opposed to *tauhid*. In Islam, there is no question of a contradiction or dualistic warfare in the world between Ahuramazda and Ahriman. The contradiction exists only in

"infinite direction," either toward clay or toward God.[3] But apart from this, in actuality man is, of course, precisely what we see in ourselves, what is examined and made known by science.

The Qur'an, moreover, repeatedly discusses the creation and composition of man in scientific, not philosophical, terms. No element of the divine essence exists in him, nor can it exist in him. God exists in man as a potentiality, a possibility, a direction in which man can strive toward God, absolute essence and infinite perfection. The profound verse "Truly we are God's and to Him we shall return" (23:60), I do not understand as referring to death and the tomb, as do the commentaries commonly in use. These commentaries imply that only when we head for the tomb does God take possession of us, when His servants come and remove us from this world that is supposedly our property. Nor do I understand it like the pantheists, who interpret it in the sense of man becoming merged in the objective essence of God, like a bubble which, bursting, is reabsorbed into the ocean; his self fades away and he becomes immortal in God. The verse does not use the word *fihi* ("in Him"); it uses the word *ilayhi* ("to Him"). That is, we return *to* God, not *in* God; the verse is proposing an orientation of man toward infinite perfection.

On account of his dualistic and contradictory nature, man, this dialectical phenomenon, is compelled to be always in motion. His own self is the stage for a battle between two forces that results in a continuous evolution toward perfection.

---

man. Satan is not the antithesis of Allah; he is His impotent and submissive creature, permitted by God to engage in enmity with man. In other words, Satan has no independent power of himself. He is the antithesis of the divine half of man, and the struggle between light and darkness, Allah and Iblis, plays itself out in the world of men, in societies and individuals; the combination Allah-Iblis yields man as its result. The world of nature is the undisputed realm of God's absolute sovereignty; it is all light, goodness and beauty. The contradiction of good and evil does not exist there, and Ahriman counts for nothing.

[3] There exists a certain apparent similarity between some of my expressions and terminology and the words used by the Sufis, the Indian and Platonic sages, and certain of the Islamic theologians . . . . What I have to say, however, should not be confused with their view . . . .

This movement is from clay toward God, but where is God? God is in infinity. Man, then, can never attain a final resting place and take up residence in God. The distance between clay and God is the distance that man travels in his search for perfection; but he travels unceasingly, in ascent and upward striving to Him Who is infinite, unbounded and unlimited. Thus the movement of man is from infinite lowliness toward infinite exaltation, and the destination is God, the spirit of God, eternity; it is impossible for him ever to stop!

How disgraceful, then, are all fixed standards. Who can ever fix a standard? Man is a "choice," a struggle, a constant becoming. He is an infinite migration, a migration within himself, from clay to God; he is a migrant within his own soul.

The path that has been laid down from clay to God is called "religion." Now we all know that religion (*madhhab*) means path, not aim; it is a road, a means.[4] All the misfortunes that are observable in religious societies arise from the fact that religion has changed its spirit and direction; its role has changed so that religion has become an aim in itself. If you turn the road into an aim or destination—work on it, adorn it, even worship it generation after generation for hundreds of years, love it and become infatuated with it so that every time its name is mentioned or your eye glimpses it you burst into tears; if you go to war with anyone who looks askance at it, spend all your time and money on decorating, repairing and leveling it, never leave it for even a minute to go in pursuit of your worldly affairs, constantly walk on it, talk about it, and rub its dust into your eyes as if it were some cure—if you do all of this, generation after generation, for hundreds of years, what will you become? You will become lost! Yes, this straight, true and correct road will deflect you and hold you back your aim and destination. And to be lost in this fashion after having found the road is worse than never to have found the road in the first place.

You have heard that this true, straight path, this smooth and sacred highway, has led thousands of men to their destination.

---

[4] The word *madhhab* is used in Persian to mean "religion" as well as "school of thought," its customary meaning in Arabic. (Tr.)

But you it has detained for a whole lifetime, so that in effect you have become like those who have chosen the wrong path which leads them astray and into misguidance.

Why? Because you have made the path a place of recreation; you have turned the highway into some sort of sacred park or clubhouse. Look at the Shi'a. In their belief, the Imam is a person who leads and guides them. But he has become for them, in effect, a sacred and invisible essence, a suprahuman entity to be praised and loved and worshipped and extolled, but nothing else! Religion as a whole, the principles and ordinances of the law, the personages important in religion—they have all become aims in themselves, and are no longer capable of directing you to the true aim and destination. Now prayer is a means; the Qur'an describes it as a means for preventing abomination and evil. But now the words and motions of prayer have become ends in themselves, so that while our knowledge of prayer has become more complex, more sensitive, more technical, the actual effectiveness of our prayer has decreased.

In my view, it is not fortuitous that all the names and expressions used in the vocabulary of Islam to designate the different aspects and dimensions of religion have the meaning of road. The word *din* (religion) itself has the meaning of road, in addition to the other significances that have been proposed for it, such as sacred wisdom and so forth. Other terms also have the same meaning: *silk:* a narrow mountain path; *shari'at:* the path leading down to a river, enabling the thirsty to take water; *tariqa:* a broad path or road leading from one town to another or one land to another; *madhhab:* a highway; *sirat:* a road leading to a place of worship; *umma:* a group of people moving toward a common destination under a single leader and along a single road.

Religion is, therefore, a road or a path, leading from clay to God and conveying man from vileness, stagnation and ignorance, from the lowly life of clay and satanic character, toward exaltation, motion, vision, the life of the spirit and divine character. If it succeeds in doing so, then it is religion in truth. But if it does not, then either you have chosen the wrong path, or you are making wrong use of the right path. In either case, the result will be the same. We see there is no difference here between Muslim and non-Muslim; neither of them attains the goal of the path.

Here someone might say, "Non-Muslims are in fact better situated than Muslims in today's world." This is true. If somebody advances with determination on an incorrect path, he may attain his goal more quickly than somebody who does not know how to make correct use of the right path. If somebody chooses a roundabout, twisting road but walks swiftly along it, he will sooner or later reach his goal. As for the people who are supposedly on the right path, either they are not walking correctly, or they are shuffling along. Maybe they are even sitting down and discussing the merits of the road! Or maybe they are simply walking around in circles, gazing admiringly on themselves; this is an even worse possibility. There are a thousand and one proofs for the correctness and the truth of the path they have chosen, and a thousand and one examples of men before them who have traversed this path and attained the destination. But despite all these signs and proofs, all this certainty and assurance, they have no awareness of their backwardness, no self-doubt, no concern to do something in order to change themselves, to see where the fault lies. Thus it is that the worshippers of cows have outpaced the worshippers of God, and our pious believers are not even aware of it.

The totality of elements that emerge from the story of Adam in the Qur'an for a comprehensive definition of Adam are, then, the following: man is a theomorphic being in exile, the combination of two opposites, a dialectical phenomenon composed of the opposition "God-Satan" or "spirit-clay." He is a free will, capable of fashioning his own destiny, responsible, committed; he accepts the unique trust of God, and receives the prostration of the angels; he is God's viceregent on earth, but also a rebel against Him; he eats the forbidden fruit of vision; and he is expelled from the garden and banished to this wasteland of nature, with the three aspects of love (= Eve), intellect (= Satan), and rebellion (= the forbidden fruit). He is commanded to create a human paradise in nature, his place of exile. He is in constant struggle within himself, striving to rise from clay to God, to ascend, so that this animal made of mud and sediment can take on the characteristics of God!

Translated from Islamshinasi, *Vol. I, pp. 68-85.*

The Philosophy of History: Cain and Abel

ACCORDING TO THE ISLAMIC school of thought, the philosophy of history is based on a certain kind of historical determinism. History represents an unbroken flow of events that, like man himself, is dominated by a dialectical contradiction, a constant warfare between two hostile and contradictory elements that began with the creation of humanity and has been waged at all places and at all times, and the sum total of which constitutes history. History is the movement of the human species along the course laid down by time, and the human species itself is a microcosm, representing the most perfect expression of being, the most evident manifestation of creation. In it, nature attains to awareness of self, and it moves toward perfection as man himself advances—nature, living, conscious and aware.

To put it differently, man is a manifestation of God's will, the absolute will and consciousness of all being, and man, according to anthropology, is the representative of God in the world, His viceregent upon earth. The history of man, which consists of the record of man's becoming and the formation of his essence, cannot therefore be accidental, something fashioned by events, the plaything of adventurers, banal, vain, aimless, purposeless and meaningless.

History is without doubt a reality, just like the other realities in the world. It began at a certain point, and must inevitably end at a certain point. It must have an aim and a direction.

Where did it begin? Like man himself, with the beginning of the contradiction!

97

In our discussion of anthropology, we have seen that man is a compound of clay and divine spirit; this is apparent from the story of Adam. The story of Adam is also the story of man, man in the real and philosophical meaning of the word. Man begins with the struggle between spirit and clay, God and Satan, within Adam. But where does history begin? What is its point of departure? The struggle between Cain and Abel.[1]

The sons of Adam were both men, human and natural, but they were at war with each other. One killed the other, and the history of humanity began. The war of Adam was a subjective, inner one that took place within his own essence (or the human race as a whole), but the war between his two sons was an objective one that took place in outer life. The story of Cain and Abel is therefore the source for our philosophy of history, just as that of Adam is the source for our philosophy of man. The war between Cain and Abel is the war between two opposing fronts that have existed throughout history, in the form of a historical dialectic. History, therefore, like man himself, consists of a dialectical process. The contradiction begins with the killing of Abel by Cain. Now Abel, in my opinion, represents the age of a pasture-based economy, of the primitive socialism that preceded ownership, and Cain represents the system of agriculture, and individual or monopoly ownership. Thereafter a permanent war began so that the whole of history became the stage for a struggle between the party of Cain the killer, and Abel, his victim, or, in other words, the ruler and the ruled. Abel the pastoralist was killed by Cain the landowner; the period of common ownership of the sources of production—the age of

[1] In this and the following section, Shari'ati is basing his theories not only on the elliptic narrative of the Qur'an (5:30-34), which does not even mention the names of Adam's sons, but also on the traditions that sprang up in amplification and explanation of the Qur'anic account. It is said that both Abel and Cain had twin sisters, and Adam decided that each should marry the other's twin sister. But Cain regarded his own twin sister as more beautiful than Abel's and therefore determined to marry her, not shrinking even from the murder of his brother in order to gain his wish. Some writers, viewing this primordial incest with repugnance, have suggested that the two brothers' brides were jinn, not human. See Tabari, *Tarikh al-Rusul wa-l-Umam*, I, pp. 137 ff; Tha'alibi, *Qisas al-Anbiya*, pp. 34-37. (TR.)

pastoralism, hunting and fishing—the spirit of brotherhood and true faith, came to an end and was replaced by the age of agriculture and the establishment of the system of private ownership, together with religious trickery and transgression against the rights of others. Abel disappeared, and Cain came to the forefront of history, and there he still lives.

I have deduced the foregoing from the fact that when Adam proposes to his sons that they should each offer a sacrifice to God in order to resolve their dispute—Cain having fallen in love with the beautiful betrothed of his brother—Cain places a handful of withered yellow corn on the altar, while Abel brings a young and valuable red-haired camel. I have therefore considered the latter as representative of pastoralism and the former as representative of agriculture. History tells us that in the age of pastoralism, which was also the age of fishing and hunting, nature was the source of all production (and in the story the camel represents this system of production). Forests, seas, deserts and rivers—these resources were at the disposal of the whole tribe, and the tools of production were mostly men's hands and arms. If in addition to these they had a few simple tools, they were objects anyone could make and own.

Monopolistic or individual ownership of the sources of production (water and land) or the tools of production (cows, plows, etc.) did not exist. Everything was equally at the disposal of everyone. The spirit and the norms of society, paternal respect, steadfastness in fulfilling moral obligations, absolute and inviolable obedience to the limitations of collective life, innate purity and sincerity of the religious conscience, a pacific spirit of love and forebearance—these were among the moral characteristics of man in that system of production, and we may take Abel as representative of them.

When man made the acquaintance of agriculture, his life, society and whole make-up became exposed to a profound revolution, which, in my view, constitutes the greatest revolution in history. It was a revolution that produced a new man, a powerful and evil man, as well as the age of civilization and discrimination.

The agricultural system resulted in a restricting of the sources of production present in nature. It brought about the emergence of advanced tools of production, complex relations of production; and since arable land, unlike forests and seas, could not be freely at the disposition of all, the need appeared for the first time in human life for men to arrogate part of nature to their own selves and deprive others of it—in a word, private ownership.

Before this, the individual had not existed in human society; the tribe itself was the individual. But now, with the coming of agriculture, that unitary society, where all men were like the brothers in a single household, was divided. The first day that a piece of land that had been owned in common was taken from nature and became the exclusive right of one person to the exclusion of all others, no law yet existed under the name of law, religion or inheritance; it was purely a matter of force. The strength of the more powerful members of the tribe in the system of pastoral ownership had served to protect the tribe and to increase its social prestige, or its sustenance from hunting and fishing; it fulfilled both of these functions for the sake of the tribe. But now it became the sole source for the determination of "rights," the measure of private consumption, and the primary factor in the acquisition of private ownership. At this critical point in history, the exact opposite of Marx's theory applies; it is not ownership that is a factor in the acquisition of power, but the converse. Power and coercion were the factor that first bestowed ownership on the individual. Power brought about private ownership, and then in turn, private ownership bestowed permanence on power and strengthened it by making it something legal and natural.

Private ownership bisected the unitary society. When acquisition and private possession became the norm, nobody was willing to content himself abstemiously with the amount he genuinely needed. In any event, it was left to every individual to determine the extent of his need. People therefore ceased the practice of acquiring property when they were obliged to rather than when they wished to. By contrast, under the previous system, the system of Abel or of collective ownership, men had engaged in hunting and fishing only to the extent of their needs. Nature, free and generous, was always at their disposal. Labor was merely a means for the satisfaction of need, and whoever was more skilled in production gained more. But now the open and abundant spread of nature—its forests and seas— had been left behind and men crowded around the poverty-stricken and pitiable meal offered them by tillage and land. In greed and acquisitiveness they began to struggle with each other. In this new form of social life, the eagles and the vultures—the crows, in the story of Cain—broke the wings of the weaker birds and drove them away. Previously, society had been like a flock of migratory birds, moving across deserts and down river banks and the shores of the oceans in harmony and unison. But now for the sake of the carrion of private property and the desire of monopoly, the birds, full of savage hatred for each other, were pecking and clawing at each other.

Finally, the human family that had been overflowing with freedom, peace, tranquillity and vitality, became transformed into two warring and contradictory camps. On one side was a minority that possessed land in excess of need and in excess of its ability to work it, and that therefore needed the labor of others. On the other side was a majority that, on the contrary, possessed only hunger and the ability to work, but had neither land nor tools. Under the new social system, the fate of the majority was clear—slavery. The class now subjected to slavery had nothing—no land, no water, no honor, no ancestry, no morality, no dignity, no thought, no art, no learning, no value, no rights, no truth, no spirit, no meaning, no education—in short, nothing in this world or the next.

For all these things of which they were deprived depended on land and the soil, on the fruits that orchards and fields yielded. These things were therefore the monopoly of the class that possessed the sources of production, not only material but also non-material. The class that did not perform menial tasks had the opportunity and capital needed to engage in education and the cultivation of abstract culture, literature, science and the arts. The two opposing classes used to live in a uniform society, animated by a single spirit, a single sentiment, a single concept of honor and dignity—that of the tribe. They used to venture together into the forest empty-handed, and out to the ocean. The riches of nature, like the air surrounding them which they inhaled together, or like the landscapes encompassing them which they beheld together, were at the disposal of both of them, at the disposal of the tribe. They were equal with each other, and therefore they were brothers. They were both sons of Adam, and Adam was from clay. Now, because of the carrion of property, they had drawn apart and were facing each other in hostility, and enmity prevailed between them. The ties of kinship had been replaced by the bonds of servitude; equality had been sacrified to discrimination, and brotherhood, to fratricide. Religion had become a means of deception and the acquisition of material benefit, and nothing else. The spirit of humanity, conciliatoriness, and compassion, gave way to the spirit of hatred, rivalry, the worship of wealth, acquisitiveness, desire for monopoly, deception, coercion, oppression, self-worship, cruelty, murderousness, transgression, the desire for domination, the claim of superiority, the creation of privilege, the despising of men, the killing of the weak, the trampling underfoot of everything and everyone for the sake of property, the killing of brothers, the torturing of fathers, and even the deceiving of God.

We can thus attain a profound understanding of the contradiction between the two types—Abel, the man of faith, peaceable and self-sacrificing, and Cain, the worshipper of passions, the transgressor, the fratricide—by means of psychological analysis and on the basis of a scientific and sociological examination of their environment, their occupations and their class. We know that they had in common their race, their father and mother, their upbringing and family, their environment and religion. In that original environment, we assume that human society had not yet been fully formed, and that different intellectual environments, varying cultural atmospheres and social groups had not yet come into being. We cannot therefore say that each of the two brothers was subject to the influence of differing religious or educational factors, at least not to the extent that they should have grown up as exact opposites, each symbolizing a certain type.

Both scientific and logical method demand that when two phenomena, though similar in every respect, develop in differing or opposing directions, we should draw up a list of all the causes, factors and conditions that affect each of them. We will then be able to delete all that they hold in common and arrive at the factor or factors that are in opposition or contradiction. The only factor that differentiates the two brothers from each other in the story consists of their different occupations. These differing occupations set the two brothers in a particular economic and social position; they have contradictory types of work, structures of production, and economic systems.

Our theory is clearly supported by the exact correspondence, on the one hand, between the type of Abel and the class psychology and the social behavior of man in the period of primitive socialism, of free pastoral hunting and fishing economy; and on the other hand, between the type of Cain and the social and class characteristics of man in the period of class society, the system of slavery and master psychology.

Now the commentators on the Qur'an and other religious scholars have said in explanation of the narrative concerning Cain and Abel that the purpose for its revelation was the condemnation of murder. But this is very superficial and oversimplifies the matter. Even if my theory is not correct, the narrative of the two brothers cannot be as slight in meaning and purpose as they hold it to be. The Abrahamic religions, especially Islam, depict this story as the first great event that occurs on the threshold of human life in this world. It is not credible that their only purpose in so doing should be the mere condemnation of murder. Whatever may be the underlying sense of the narrative, it is surely far more than a simple ethical tale, yielding the conclusion, "It has thus become clear to us now that murder is an evil deed, so we must try never to commit this shameful act. Let us avoid doing it, particularly to our brothers!"

In my opinion, the murder of Abel at the hands of Cain represents a great development, a sudden swerve in the course of history, the most important event to have occurred in all human life. It interprets and explains that event in a most profound fashion—scientifically, sociologically, and with reference to class. The story concerns the end of primitive communism, the disappearance of man's original system of equality and brotherhood, expressed in the hunting and fishing system of productivity (equated with Abel), and its replacement by agricultural production, the creation of private ownership, the formation of the first class society, the system of discrimination and exploitation, the worship of wealth and lack of true faith, the beginning of enmity, rivalry, greed, plunder, slavery and fratricide (equated with Cain). The death of Abel and the survival of Cain are objective, historical realities, and the fact that henceforth religion, life, economy, government and the fate of men were all in the hands of Cain represents a realistic, critical and progressive analysis of what happened. Similarly, the fact that Abel died without issue and mankind today consists of the heirs of Cain[2] also means that the society, government, religion, ethics, world-view and conduct of Cain have become universal, so that the disequilibrium and instability of thought and morality that prevail in every society and every age derive from this fact.

The story of Cain and Abel depicts the first day in the life of the sons of Adam on this earth (their marriage with their sisters)[3] as being identical with the beginning of contradiction, conflict and ultimately warfare and fratricide. This confirms the scientific fact that life, society and history are based on contradiction and struggle, and that contrary to the belief of the idealists, the fundamental factors in all three are economics and sexuality, which come to predominate over religious faith, brotherly ties, truth and morality.

The source of the conflict between Cain and Abel was the following. Cain preferred the sister who had been betrothed to Abel to his own fiancee. He insisted on having her, and demanded the betrothal that had been concluded with Adam's approval be annulled. The two brothers went before Adam, who then proposed to them that they each offer a sacrifice. Whoever had his sacrifice accepted should have the sister, and

---

[2] We mean heirs in a typological sense, not a genealogical one.

[3] Certain pious believers have invented various devices for legitimizing the marriages of Cain and Abel in order to free mankind of the blemish of bastardy. However, it is a little late for that! (See our earlier footnote on p. 98. Tr.)

the loser should accept the result. Cain tried trickery, brought his trickery to bear and brought some withered corn as his sacrifice; naturally, it was not accepted. (See how Cain always practices treachery whenever he feels the need, even toward God! Every representative of the "system of Cain" behaves in the same way.) Again Cain resorted to trickery, and preferring his own passions to God's word, he vilely slaughtered Abel (who, although he was not the original complainant and desired nothing of Cain, had offered God his best camel, his most precious possession, a sacrifice which was of course accepted).

The dialogue that takes place between them at the time of Abel's death is also instructive. Cain threatens him with death, but Abel replies softly, kindly and submissively, "But I will not raise my hand against you."

The society and system represented by Abel were thus subdued by the aggressive and acquisitive system of Cain, without there being any resistance offered.

When considering the story of Cain and Abel, I wondered at first whether the question of sexuality might not be depicted in it as a stronger and more primary factor than economics. Might not Freudianism be correct in this case? The first word uttered in the conflict was, after all, "woman," just as everything began with Eve in the case of their father.

But if we think a little more deeply, we see that matters are not this simple. It is true that the first source of the conflict is Cain's attraction to the betrothed of Abel; so far, Freud would appear to be right. But were Freud to accept that another cause, or set of causes and factors, existed prior to sexuality—which he regards as the primary cause—he would have to agree that the story cannot be analyzed in the sense of primacy of the sexual factor. For before the question of sexuality arises, this question too must be considered: it is true that Cain begins the dispute with his brother on account of his attraction to his betrothed, but why does Cain of the two brothers display this type of behavior? For considering the important fact that both brothers had a similar heredity and environment, they ought to have conducted themselves in an identical manner, both showing the same

determination and steadfastness.[4] Then again, even if it be
scientifically possible that under identical conditions, only one
of the two brothers should manifest such conduct, why was that
one Cain? There is also this third point, that the general conclusion to be drawn from the text of the story and the dialogue
between the two brothers and their respective forms of behavior,
as well as the view of the narrator of the story—this being the
Qur'an, and also the Christian and more particularly Jewish
texts, not to mention books of exegesis, history and Islamic
lore—the conclusion to be drawn from all of these is that Abel is
presented as the type of good and Cain as the type of evil. I use
the word "type" and not "character," for the latter would imply
that Cain possessed only evil characteristics such as lust and
materialism, and that Abel possessed only good characteristics
such as religiosity and sensitivity. No, one of them is the complete manifestation of an evil man, and the other of a good man.

I have therefore reached the conclusion that Abel is a man of
sound disposition; an inhuman and unbalanced social system,
form of work and economic life have not alienated, disfigured,
perverted or polluted him; they have not made of him a crippled
and defective being, one of the "fractured," to use the expression of Marcuse, polluted and laden with complexes. At the
same time that he is filled with love for his father, affection for
his brother, belief in God and steadfastness for the sake of
justice, and does not display the same passionate insistence as
his brother on the fulfillment of his sexual appetites, he is not
neutral and insensitive to the face of beauty. For throughout the
various tribulations to which Cain subjects him—even threat-
ening him with death on several occasions—he did not say even
once, in pious abstention: "Here, brother, I renounce her. She's
not worth arguing over; take her, she's yours."

Abel was a man, a "son of Adam," neither more nor less. All
the texts that relate this story present him in this light. The
reason for this, in my opinion, is that he lived in a society

[4] For example, it is not possible to say that they were both brothers, but one
studied in Qum while the other studied in Paris, one read Islamic periodicals
and the other, frivolous magazines! Or that one of them had a *sayyida* for a
mother and the other, a Swede!

without contradiction and discrimination; his work was free and unfettered—"He was neither mounted on a camel, nor laden like a donkey; neither a master of slaves, nor servant to a king."[5] He was merely a man. In a society where all enjoy equally and possess in common all the bounties of life, all the material and spiritual resources of society, all will necessarily be equal and brothers, and the spirit of salubrity, beauty, kindness, purity, sincerity, love and goodness will be cultivated.

Cain is not inherently evil. His essence is the same as that of Abel, and nobody is inherently evil, for the essence of everyone is the same as the essence of Adam. What makes Cain evil is an anti-human social system, a class society, a regime of private ownership that cultivates slavery and mastery and turns men into wolves, foxes or sheep. It is a setting where hostility, rivalry, cruelty and venality flourish; humiliation and lordship —the hunger of some and the gluttony of others, greed, opulence and deception; a setting where the philosophy of life is founded on plundering, exploitation, enslavement, consuming and abusing, lying and flattering; where life consists of oppressing or being oppressed, of selfishness, aristocratic arrogance, hoarding, thievery and ostentation; where human relations are based on the giving and receiving of blows, on exploiting or being exploited; where human philosophy consists of maximum enjoyment, maximum wealth, maximum lust, and maximum coercion; where all things revolve around egoism and the sacrifice of all things to the ego, a vile, crude and avaricious ego.

It is all this that makes of Cain—the brother of good, kind, pure Abel; the immediate son of Adam—a creature ready to lie, to commit treachery, to drag his faith into the mud with a quiet conscience, and ultimately to behead his brother, all for the sake of his sexual inclinations—not even some crazed and powerful infatuation, but straightforward and transient lust! No, Mr. Freud, he does all of these things not because his sexual instincts are stronger than those of others, but because (and this is quite simple) human virtues have grown exceedingly weak in him, weaker even than some feeble expression of lust. If what

[5] A line quoted from the *Gulistan* of Sa'di. (TR.)

Freud said were true, and the sexual factor were so strong in him that he would do anything to attain the object of his desire, then he would have been the one to offer up a precious red-haired camel at the altar, not Abel! If what Freud said were true, we would see Cain running out into the fields and burning all his crops as soon as his father made the suggestion.

We see, on the contrary, that all Cain is ready to do in order to gain God's pleasure and win his lost love is to sacrifice a handful of grain, grain that was, moreover, yellowing and withered.

My purpose in examining the story in such detail has been first, to refute the idea that it is exclusively ethical in purpose, for it treats of something far more serious than the topic for a mere essay, and secondly, to make clear that it is not the story of a dispute between two brothers. Instead, it treats two wings of human society, two modes of production; it is the story of history, the tale of bifurcated humanity in all ages, the beginning of a war that is still not concluded.

The wing represented by Abel is that of the subject and the oppressed; i.e., the people, those who throughout history have been slaughtered and enslaved by the system of Cain, the system of private ownership which has gained ascendancy over human society. The war between Cain and Abel is the permanent war of history which has been waged by every generation. The banner of Cain has always been held high by the ruling classes, and the desire to avenge the blood of Abel has been inherited by succeeding generations of his descendants—the subjected people who have fought for justice, freedom and true faith in a struggle that has continued, one way or another, in every age. The weapon of Cain has been religion, and the weapon of Abel has also been religion.

It is for this reason that the war of religion against religion has also been a constant of human history. On the one hand is the religion of *shirk,* of assigning partners to God, a religion that furnishes the justification for *shirk* in society and class discrimination. On the other hand is the religion of *tauhid,* of the oneness of God, which furnishes the justification for the unity of all classes and races. The transhistorical struggle between Abel and Cain is also the struggle between *tauhid* and *shirk,* between justice and human unity on the one hand, and social and racial discrimination on the other. There has existed throughout human history, and there will continue to exist until the last day, a struggle between the religion of deceit, stupefaction and justification of the status quo and the religion of awareness, activism and revolution. The end of time will come when Cain dies and the "system of Abel" is established anew. That inevitable revolution will mean the end of the history of Cain; equality will be realized throughout the world, and human unity and brotherhood will be established, through equity and justice. This is the inevitable direction of history. A universal revolution will take place in all areas of human life; the oppressed classes of history will take their revenge. The glad tidings of God will be realized: "We have willed that We should place under obligation those who have been weakened and oppressed on the earth, by making them the leaders of men and heirs to the earth" (Qur'an, 28:5).

This inevitable revolution of the future will be the culmination of the dialectical contradiction that began with the battle of Cain and Abel and has continued to exist in all human societies, between the ruler and the ruled. The inevitable outcome of history will be the triumph of justice, equity and truth.[6]

It is the responsibility of every individual in every age to determine his stance in the constant struggle between the two wings we have described, and not to remain a spectator. While believing in a certain form of historical determinism, we believe also in the freedom of the individual and his human responsibility, which lie at the very heart of the process of historical determinism. We do not see any contradiction between the two, because history advances on the basis of a universal and scientifically demonstrable process of determinism, but "I" as an indi-

[6] Justice (*'adl*) refers mostly to the legal relations between individuals and groups, on the basis of the laws laid down in society. Equity (*qist*) refers to the equal enjoyment by all men of the fruits of their labor and of their rights, whether or not this is recognized by law. Justice implies the existence of a judicial system, and equity relates to the structure of society. In order to have justice, the judiciary must be reformed; in order to have equity, the social system must be changed—not superficially, but in its fundamental structure.

vidual human being must choose whether to move forward
with history and accelerate its determined course with the force
of knowledge and science, or to stand with ignorance, egoism,
opportunism in the face of history, and be crushed.

Translated from Islamshinasi, *Vol. I, pp. 85-94.*

The Dialectic of Sociology

SOCIOLOGY IS ALSO FOUNDED on a dialectic. Society, like history, is composed of two classes—the class of Abel and the class of Cain—for history is simply the movement of society along the line traced out by time. Society represents, therefore, a fragment corresponding to a certain time-sector in history. If we remove the concept of time from the history of a people, we will be left with the society of that people.

In my opinion, there are only two possible structures in all of human society—the structure of Cain and the structure of Abel. I do not regard slavery, serfdom, bourgeoisie, feudalism and capitalism as constituting social structures. These are all part of the superstructure of society. Marx has put all these five stages—together with a special stage he calls the Asiatic mode of production—on the same level as primitive socialism and perfected socialism (i.e., the classless society that is ultimately to come into being). He has regarded them as all belonging to the same category and designated them all as "structures." According to Marx, when the village khan becomes the urban hajji, and the peasants become workers, a change takes place in the structure of society, just like the change that occurred when the common ownership of the sources of production gave way to private ownership, with one group owning everything and another group lacking everything. To equate the two changes is remarkable!

No more than two structures can exist in society: one where society is the lord and master of its own destiny, and all men work for it and its benefit, and another in which individuals are owners, and the masters of their own destinies and the destiny of society. However, within each of these two structures, there

111

exist different modes of production, forms of relationship, tools, resources and commodities; all these constitute the "superstructure." For example, within the structure of Abel, it is possible to have economic socialism (i.e., collective owner- ship); the pastoral and hunting mode of production, and the hunting mode of production (both existed in the primitive commune); the industrial mode of production (in the classless, post-capitalist society); and even the mode of production, the tools and commodities of the period of the urban bourgeoisie; and the artisan and peasant culture of the feudal period with its socialist structure.

At the opposing pole, that of the "structure of Cain," or economic monopoly and private ownership, various economic systems, forms of class relations, and tools, types and resources of production, may also exist. Slavery, serfdom, feudalism, bourgeoisie, industrial capitalism, and—as its culmination— imperialism, all belong to the structure of Cain.

But in my opinion, Marx has mixed certain criteria in his philosophy of history, so that his classification of the stages of social development has become confused. He has confused three distinct entities: the form of ownership, the form of class relations, and the form of the tools of production. According to Marx, the stages of historical development, each of which he regards as a change in social structure, are the following:

1) Primitive socialism, the period in which society lives col- lectively and on the basis of equality, in which production consists of hunting and fishing, and there is joint ownership of the sources of production—the forests and streams, Here, the criterion of the structure is the form of ownership, which is collective.

2) Slavery, the period in which society is divided into two classes, master and slave, and the relationship between these two classes is that of owner and property, or man and animal. The master has the right to do what he wills with his slave, his tool—to kill him, beat him, or sell him. Here, the determining factor in the structure is the form of human relationship.

3) Serfdom, the period in which one class owns the land, and the other class, the serfs, although liberated from slavery to

masters, has in effect become a slave to the land and tied to it. They are bought and sold together with the land, and their status vis-a-vis the landowner is higher than that of the slave but lower than that of the peasant.

4) Feudalism, a mode of production based on agriculture and land ownership. The landowner is a master who enjoys political power over the mass of the peasants, within certain limits. He levies taxes, and possesses certain moral and inborn privileges; he possesses "honor and nobility" based on blood and lineage; he has inherited them and the masses are deprived of them.

5) Bourgeoisie, a structure based on acquisition and commerce, on handicrafts and urban life, and the exchange of money. The middle class—i.e., the class intermediate between peasant and landlord, between aristocracy and serf—the shopkeeper, the tradesman, the artisan, the urban craftsman—comes into its own, and with its newly acquired wealth, takes the place of the former aristocracy of ancient lineage and noble birth. The landlord-peasant relationship disappears, and tendencies to liberalism and democracy make their appearance.

6) The full development of the bourgeoisie and industry. Capital is accumulated and production becomes concentrated in large-scale industry. Shops give way to supermarkets, small rooms in the bazaar to companies, small artisan workshops to vast factories, moneychangers to banks, caravansarais to stock exchanges, and merchants to capitalists. In place of the exchange of money, drafts, cheques, shares and credits become the symbols of economic exchange and commercial transaction. The peasants are drawn from their fields, and the workers from their bazaars, ateliers and shops, to the factories and the poles of industrial production. There, they are placed everyday under increasing pressure. Since the means of production and the tools of labor are no longer spade, pick, saw and ax, or cow, donkey and plow, but only machinery, the worker becomes totally at the disposal of the capitalist. He faces him empty-handed, and can demand only a wage for the labor of his hand. He is more of a captive and more exploited than before. It is for this reason that he is no longer called worker, but proletarian.

7) As the capitalists become fewer in number and greater in wealth, and both industry and capital continually expand, the industrial proletariat is placed under ever-increasing pressure. But it becomes stronger at the same time, and the dialectical war between the two poles ends in the triumph of the proletariat. The private ownership of industry and capital is abolished; public ownership takes its place; and a classless society comes into being.

We can see clearly that the first and seventh stages are characterized by the same structure, as are the second, third, fourth, fifth and sixth stages. Throughout history, then, only two structures have existed, and it is not possible for there to be more than two. For example, the structure existing in feudalism and industrial capitalism is the same; in both cases we see private ownership of the tools and resources of production. Again in both cases, the social structure is based upon class; the only differences are the tools of production, the form of production, and, as a result, the outer form of the relations of production. The converse also holds true: it is possible for the tools, form and relations of production to be the same, but for the structure to be different. For example, a society that engages in agricultural production, with tools that are unchanged, that has no notion of industry or capitalism and no developed bourgeoisie, may establish a socialist structure, a system of collective ownership, by means of revolution, war with external forces or internal coup d'etat.

Once I and my fellow tribesman lived together in equality and brotherhood, hunting and fishing; a single structure existed in our society. Then he became an owner, and I, one of the deprived; he, the ruler, and I, the ruled. The form of things changed, the tools and the mode of production, but he remained an owner and did not work, and I remained one of the deprived and worked. One day, I was a slave and he was the master. Then I became a serf and he became the lord. Then I became a peasant and he became the landlord. Later still, I laid down my spade, and he abandoned his horse, and we both came to the city. He bought a few taxis with the proceeds of his land, and I became a taxi-driver. Now he has a factory, and I am the proletarian working in it! When and in what respect did the structure ever change? It was only the forms, the names, the tools, the forms of labor that changed; all these things relate to the superstructure. In all periods, with the exception of the period of primordial equality and fraternity, he retained his position of ruler and I, my position of ruled, running back and forth in his service. The structure will change only when we again both go out to work on the same piece of land as before, with the same cow, plow and spade as before!

It is possible, then, to divide society in accordance with these two structures, into two poles, the "pole of Cain" and the "pole of Abel."

1) The pole of Cain. The ruler = king, owner, aristocracy. In the primitive and backward stages of social development, this pole is represented by a single individual, a single force that exercises power and absorbs all three powers (king, owner and aristocracy) into itself; it represents a single visage, the visage of Cain. But at later stages in the development and evolution of the social system, of civilization and culture, and the growth of the different dimensions of social life and the class structure, this pole acquires three separate dimensions and presents itself under three different aspects. It has a political manifestation— power, an economic manifestation—wealth, and a religious manifestation—asceticism.

In the Qur'an, the Pharaoh is the symbol of the ruling political power; Croesus (Qarun) is the symbol of the ruling economic power; and Balaam is the symbol of the official, ruling clergy. They are the threefold manifestation of the single Cain.

These three manifestations are referred to in the Qur'an as *mala'*, *mutraf* and *rahib*, meaning, respectively, the avaricious and brutal, the gluttons and the overfed, and the official clergy, the long-bearded demagogues. These three classes are constantly engaged in, respectively, dominating, exploiting and deceiving the people.[1]

---

[1] Islam has abolished all forms of official mediation between God and man, and the Qu'ran mentions the third manifestation of Cain—the official clergy— with harsh words, even going so far as to curse them and compare them to donkeys and dogs. The Prophet of Islam said: "Any beard longer than a man's

2) The pole of Abel. The ruled = God-the people. Confronting the threefold class of king-owner-aristocracy is the class of the people, *al-nas*. The two classes have opposed and confronted each other throughout history. In the class society, Allah stands in the same rank as *al-nas*, in such a fashion that wherever in the Qur'an social matters are mentioned, Allah and *al-nas* are virtually synonymous. The two words are often interchangeable, and yield the same meaning.

For example, in the verse beginning "If ye lend Allah a goodly loan . . . ." (Qur'an, 64:17), it is obvious that what is meant by God is in reality "people," for God has no need of any loans from you.

In the affairs of society, therefore, in all that concerns the social system, but not in credal matters such as the order of the cosmos, the words *al-nas* and *Allah* belong together. Thus when it is said, "Rule belongs to God," the meaning is that rule belongs to the people, not to those who present themselves as the representatives or the sons of God, as God Himself or as one of His close relatives. When it is said, "Property belongs to God," the meaning is that capital belongs to the people as a

---

hand shall be in hellfire," and he also commanded men to keep short their sleeves and the hems of their garments. All of this is a sign of the struggle that Islam has waged against the concept of an official clergy that exists in all other religions, and the attention it has paid to their deviationist role in stupefying the people and distorting the truth. What is important to remember is that Islam has no clergy; the word "clergy" (*ruhaniyun*) is recent, a borrowing from Christianity. We have scholars of religion; they do not constitute official authorities who impose themselves by way of heredity or monopolistic powers. They are simply specialized scholars who have come into being in Islamic society as the result of a necessity, not on an institutionalized basis. They derive their influence, presence and power in society from the people and the free and natural choice of the members of society. They are normal individuals, either students who piously study religion with effort and the endurance of hardship, or scholars who teach and conduct research. If their ranks have been penetrated by the illiterate, this is because of the general illiteracy of society or other factors. The garb they wear is not that of an official clergy, but that of knowledge, personal investigation and research.

whole, not to Croesus.[2] When it is said, "Religion belongs to God," the meaning is that the entire structure and content of religion belongs to the people; it is not a monopoly held by a certain institution or certain people known as "clergy" or "church."

The word "people" (*al-nas*) has a profound meaning and distinct significance in Islam. It is only the people as a whole who are the representatives of God and His "family" (*al-nas iyalu 'Llah*). The Qur'an begins in the name of God and ends in the name of the people. The Ka'ba is the House of God, but the Qur'an also calls it the "house of the people" and the "free house" (*al-bayt al-'atiq*) (22:29, 33), as opposed to other houses that are in the bond of private ownership. We see here that the word *al-nas* does not denote a mere collection of individuals. On the contrary, it has the sense of "society" as opposed to "individuals." The word *al-nas* is a singular noun with the sense of a plural; it is a word without a singular. What word could better convey the concept of "society," something possessed of an identity totally independent from all of its individual members.

All societies that have existed throughout history, whether they have been defined in national, political or economic terms, have been founded on a system of contradiction, a contradiction that has existed at its very heart. Within every class society, two

[2] Mu'awiya said, "Property belongs to God," and Abu Dharr retorted, "You say this in order to draw the conclusion that since I am the representative of God, property belongs to me. Say instead, 'Property belongs to the people.' " The celebrated dictum "People are empowered over their own property," from which the principle of *taslit* ("empowering") in Islamic jurisprudence has been derived, means exactly the opposite of what is commonly thought. People have regarded it as constituting a religious justification for individual ownership and the sanctity of private capital. They have interpreted "people" as meaning "individuals," whereas on the contrary, what is intended is "people's ownership" of property, as opposed to the ownership of those individuals who have gained control of the wealth of the people through plunder, usurpation, exploitation, whether "legally" or "illegally"! The subsequent addition of the word "and their own persons" at the end of the hadith may have had the purpose of further reinforcing the concept of individuality at the expense of that of *al-nas*.

hostile and opposing classes have existed: on the one hand, king, owner and aristocracy, and on the other, God and the people.[3] On the one hand, religions in their multiplicity; on the other, the one religion.

---

[3] According to the Qur'an (94:1-3), Allah is the Lord of the People, King of the People, and the God of the People. That is, He does not belong to the aristocracy, to the prominent minority in society, to the elite. Note carefully these three concepts relating to Allah and His relationship with men, as well as the opposites implied by each of them.

Translated from Islamshinasi, *Vol. I, pp. 97-98.*

The Ideal Society—the Umma

THE IDEAL SOCIETY OF ISLAM is called the *umma*. Taking the place of all the similar concepts which in different languages and cultures designate a human agglomeration or society, such as "society," "nation," "race," "people," "tribe," "clan," etc., is the single word *umma*, a word imbued with progressive spirit and implying a dynamic, committed and ideological social vision.

The word *umma* derives from the root *amm*, which has the sense of path and intention. The *umma* is, therefore, a society in which a number of individuals, possessing a common faith and goal, come together in harmony with the intention of advancing and moving toward their common goal.

While other expressions denoting human agglomerations have taken unity of blood or soil and the sharing of material benefit as the criterion of society, Islam, by choosing the word *umma*, has made intellectual responsibility and shared movement toward a common goal the basis of its social philosophy.

The infrastructure of the *umma* is the economy, because "Whoever has no worldly life has no spiritual life." Its social system is based on equity and justice and ownership by the people, on the revival of the "system of Abel," the society of human equality and thus also of brotherhood—the classless society. This is a fundamental principle, but it is not the aim, as in Western socialism, which has retained the world-view of the Western bourgeoisie. The political philosophy and the form of regime of the *umma* is not the democracy of heads, not irresponsible and directionless liberalism which is a plaything of contesting social forces, not putrid aristocracy, not anti-popular dictatorship, not a self-imposing oligarchy. It consists rather of "purity of leadership" (not the leader, for that would be fascism), committed and revolutionary leadership, responsible for the movement and growth of society on the basis of its world-view and ideology, and for the realization of the divine destiny of man in the plan of creation. This is the true meaning of imamate!

Translated from Islamshinasi, *Vol I, pp. 98-104.*

The Ideal Man—
The Viceregent of God

THE IDEAL MAN IS the theomorphic man in whom the spirit of God has overcome the half of his being that relates to Iblis, to clay and to sediment. He has been freed from hesitation and the contradiction between the "two infinites." "Take on the characteristics of God"—this is our whole philosophy of education, our sole standard! For it is a negation of all fixed and conventional standards in favor of assuming the characteristics and attributes of God. It is a progression toward the absolute goal and absolute perfection, an eternal and infinite evolution, not a molding in stereotyped forms of uniform men.

This man, the man that ought to be but is not, is a bi-dimensional man, a bird capable of flying with both wings. He is not the man of those cultures and civilizations that cultivate good men and powerful men separately from each other—on the one hand, men pure and pious but with weak consciousness and awareness, and on the other hand, powerful and brilliant geniuses, but with narrow hearts and hands polluted by sin. There are, on the one hand, men whose hearts are devoted to the inner life, to beauty and the mysteries of the spirit, but whose lives are spent in poverty, decline, humiliation and weakness, like those hundreds of thousands of Indian ascetics who despite their spirituality, their inner wonders, their subtle and exalted feelings, were for long years the playthings and wretched prisoners of a handful of English colonels. On the other hand, there are men who fend the earth, the mountains, the sea and the heavens, with the power of their industry, who create a life overflowing with abundance, enjoyment and prosperity, but in whom feeling and all sense of value have been suspended, and

121

the peculiarly human capacity to perceive the spirit of the world, the profundity of life, the creation of beauty, and the belief in something higher than nature and history has been weakened or paralyzed.

Ideal man passes through the very midst of nature and comes to understand God; he seeks out mankind and thus attains God. He does not bypass nature and turn his back on mankind. He holds the sword of Caesar in his hand and he has the heart of Jesus in his breast. He thinks with the brain of Socrates and loves God with the heart of Hallaj. As Alexis Carrel desired, he is a man who understands the beauty of science and the beauty of God; he listens to the words of Pascal and the words of Descartes.

Like the Buddha, he is delivered from the dungeon of pleasure-seeking and egoism; like Lao Tse, he reflects on the profundity of his primordial nature; and like Confucius, he meditates on the fate of society.

Like Spartacus, he is a rebel against slaveowners, and like Abu Dharr, he scatters the seed for the revolution of the hungry.

Like Jesus, he bears a message of love and reconciliation, and like Moses, he is the messenger of jihad and deliverance.

He is a man whom philosophical thought does not make inattentive to the fate of mankind, and whose involvement in politics does not lead to demagoguery and fame-seeking. Science has not deprived him of the taste of faith, and faith has not paralyzed his power of thought and logical deduction. Piety has not made of him a harmless ascetic, and activism and commitment have not stained his hands with immorality. He is a man of jihad and ijtihad, of poetry and the sword, of solitude and commitment, of emotion and genius, of strength and love, of faith and knowledge. He is a man uniting all the dimensions of true humanity. He is a man whom life has not made a one-dimensional, fractured and defeated creature, alienated from his own self. Through servitude to God, he has delivered himself from servitude to things and to people, and his submission to the absolute will of God has summoned him to rebellion against all forms of compulsion. He is a man who has dissolved his transient individuality in the eternal identity of the human race, who through the negation of self becomes everlasting.

He has accepted the heavy Trust of God, and for this very reason, he is a responsible and committed being, with the free exercise of his will. He does not perceive his perfection as lying in the creation of a private relationship with God, to the exclusion of men; it is, rather, in struggle for the perfection of the human race, in enduring hardship, hunger, deprivation and torment for the sake of the liberty, livelihood and well-being of men, in the furnace of intellectual and social struggle, that he attains piety, perfection and closeness to God.

He is not a man who has been formed by his environment; on the contrary, it is he who has formed his environment. He has delivered himself from all the forms of compulsion that constantly press down upon man and impose their stereotypes on him by means of science, technology, sociology and self-awareness, through faith and awareness. He is free of the compulsion of nature and heredity, the compulsion of history, the compulsion of society and environment; guided by science and technology, he has freed himself from these three prisons. As for the fourth prison, that of the self, he has liberated himself from it by means of love. He has rebelled against the ego, subdued it and refashioned it.

Liberating his character from the inherited norms of his race and the conventions of his society—all of which are relative and the product of environment—and discovering eternal and divine values, he takes on the characteristics of God and attains the nature of the absolute. He no longer acts virtuously as a duty imposed upon him, and his ethics are no longer a collection of restraints forced upon him by the social conscience. To be good has become identical with his nature, and exalted values are the fundamental components of his essence; they are inherent to his being, his living, his thinking, his loving.

Art is not a plaything in his hands; it is not a means for gaining pleasure, for diversion, for stupefaction, for the expenditure of accumulated energy. It is not a servant to sexuality, politics or capital. Art is the special trust given to man by God. It is the creative pen of the Maker, given by Him to his viceregent so that he might make a second earth and a second paradise, new forms of life, beauty, thought, spirit, message, a new heaven, a new time. God possesses absolute freedom, absolute awareness and absolute creative power. Ideal man, the bearer of God's trust, he whom God has fashioned in His own form, is an eternal will overflowing with beauty, virtue and wisdom. In all of nature, only man has attained to a relative freedom, a relative awareness, and a relative creative power. For God created him in His own image and made of him His relative, telling him, "If you seek Me, take your own self as an indication."

Ideal man has three aspects: truth, goodness and beauty—in other words, knowledge, ethics and art.

In nature, he is the viceregent of God; he is a committed will with the three dimensions of awareness, freedom and creativity.

He is a theomorphic being exiled on earth; with the combined wealth of love and knowledge, he rules over all beings; in front of him, the angels prostrate themselves.

He is the great rebel of the world. His existence is a smooth path trodden by the will of God, Who desires to accomplish the ultimate purpose of His creation in him and by him. He has descended from the paradise of nature to the desert of self-awareness and exile to create there the paradise of man.

He who is now the viceregent of God has traversed the difficult path of servitude, and carrying the burden of the Trust, he has now come to the end of history and the last frontier of nature.

Resurrection is about to begin, and a project unfolds among God, man and love, a project for the creation of a new world, for telling the tale of a new creation.

Thus it was that the Trust God proposed to the earth, the heavens and the mountains, they all forebore from assuming; it was only man that accepted it.

Man, this rebel against God
Who has given one hand to the devil—intellect
And the other hand to Eve—love,
Who bears on his back the heavy burden of the Trust,
Descended from the paradise of painless enjoyment,
Alone and a stranger in this world.
He is a rebel, but constantly yearning to return,

And now he has learned through worship how to
     attain the path of salvation.
And through submission to the constraints of the beloved,
After escaping blind constraint through his rebellion,
He is now delivered too from the torment of the escape
     of desperation.
He who fled from God
Was tested and purged in the furnaces of this world—
Awareness, solitude, decision—
And now he knows
The path of return toward God,
That great Friend Who is awaiting him,
The path that leads to Him by becoming Him.

Index